Excel
AT LIVING

A

CENTERED
LIFE

Excel

AT LIVING

A

CENTERED
LIFE

HOWARD LULL

TATE PUBLISHING *& Enterprises*

Published by Tate Publishing & Enterprises, LLC
127 E. Trade Center Terrace | Mustang, Oklahoma 73064 USA
1.888.361.9473 | www.tatepublishing.com

Tate Publishing is committed to excellence in the publishing industry. The company reflects the philosophy established by the founders, based on Psalms 68:11,
"The Lord gave the word and great was the company of those who published it."

Book design copyright © 2007 by Tate Publishing, LLC. All rights reserved.
Cover design by Melanie Harr-Hughes
Interior design by Lindsay B. Behrens

Published in the United States of America

ISBN: 1-59886-08-5-2
07.10.05

DEDICATIONS

I choose to dedicate this book to all the wonderful people I have met and have yet to meet who desire to become all they can be in every area of their life. I dedicate this book to those who dare to dream and take risks few others dare to take.

More importantly, I dedicate this book to my Heavenly Father and His Son who have been a Father to the Fatherless and have loved all of humanity in ways we have never understood.

Acknowledgments

Writing this book has been an educational experience I have been blessed to receive. I want every person who has contributed, whether in encouraging support or technical support, to know you have been invaluable to me, and most importantly, I honor our relationship. I want to thank Tate Publishing for their expertise and inviting me into their publishing family. I want to thank my immediate family, Brenda, Jacqueline and Zachary who always believed in me and added so much joy to my life. I also thank my mom, JoAnn Crowder, who has been faithfully praying for all her children to reach their eternal destinations in Christ. I love you, Mom. I want to thank George and Mary Lou Grier who loved me as a son-in-law as if I was their own son. Their love was a true investment in my life.

I want to thank Ed Simpson, my brother-in-law, who listened to me and gave me support to continue to fight the good fight of faith. Even knowing me as well as he does, he still desires to be my friend. I want to thank Lowell C. Kruse, whom I believe is one of the best CEOs in healthcare. He has taught me much about navigating my way through the business. Yes, I acknowledge I am partly responsible for some of his hair loss, but he still hung with me. I want to thank Dr. Gordon Brown at the University of Missouri who believes in his students and the process and the contribution he knows we will make before we have ever made the contribution. I want to thank Dr. Ann Sedore who has a heart for people and nurses everywhere. She gave me a great opportunity to use my skills in investing in people at Upstate Medical University in Syracuse, New York. I want to acknowledge John G. Miller, author of the *QBQ! The Question behind the Question* for encouraging me, sharing his insights with me, and teaching others to take personal accountability.

I desire to thank Dr. Michael Dunlap who encouraged and supported me in my first job as an emergency department nurse and still takes interest in my career. I want to thank Dr. Edward Andres, a great trauma surgeon, who had the patience and vision to allow me to succeed as a trauma coordinator and gain invaluable insights into treating trauma patients and their families. I am thankful to Dr. Richard Hunt at the Center for Disease Control in Atlanta for entrusting me with his emergency department and helping me to make things better during his tenure at Upstate. I want to acknowledge every trauma nurse and paramedic, for I do know the investment you make in the lives of others and the price you pay to do it.

I want to thank Pastor Brian Zahnd of Word of Life Church in St. Joseph, Missouri for his encouragement as I have watched him fulfill his destiny. I am truly thankful and desire to acknowledge Pastor John Carter of Abundant Life Christian Center in Syracuse, New York, for his passion for investing in people. I want to acknowledge Rick Hartigan and Kevin Bocquin who made it their goal to run me in the ground when training for marathons, all the while listening to all my philosophies of life, which I have included in this writing. They helped make me a better runner. I helped them learn to tune people out when listening to philosophy. If I listed everyone to whom I am truly thankful, this book wouldn't be big enough.

However, it's in listing this wide array of people that you may see them as gifts that God deposited in my life, for all of them and all of you who are readers and investors in my life, I am truly thankful.

TABLE OF CONTENTS

How to read this book:

I want you to read this book just as if you and I are sitting together having a hot cup of coffee, chatting about life, and sharing and comparing our insights as well as our successes and failures. We will laugh about some, shed a tear about some, and yet, we will come away encouraged, deciding to passionately pursue life. I want you to enjoy the uniqueness in which God has designed me and yet still uses me to impart his wisdom in that unique way. I guarantee you some will be shocked as they read this book and learn that I believe the way I do. I encourage you to use a highlighter and mark the passages from which you gain insight and knowledge. Please share these insights with others and build upon them, and in turn teach me as well. I want to continue learning and developing ways to live a centered life. I divided this book into chapters simply to give reference points.

1

The Beginning

I am a student of life. I love living life. Life around me is never dull. I love each new day and the opportunities it brings with it. Even though I love life, I have found it difficult to manage at times. I am sure you can relate to that. I have learned that when one area of my life is out of order, it affects all other areas to varying degrees. It was necessary for me to learn to become centered and to excel at living a centered life so that I may know which area of my life keeps all the other areas in order. I also have found the importance of correcting any area that is not centered and may be throwing my life out of balance. I love being around people, but I wasn't always like this. There was a period in my life of anger and hurt, which you will read about as you go on this journey with me. Before we get much further, you need to know that I am a Christian. Everything I do and write comes out of that value system. That being said, this book contains some very practical ways to live a centered life.

Being centered, I now invest in people. I help people to focus and center their lives on what is most important to them. We all have drivers in our lives. Most of us have more than one driver. Things drive us like our love for people, money, and success. All of these are good things when given their proper place in our lives. We just need to learn to identify the drivers and keep them centered.

I believe that people are the greatest resource this world has to offer. People are God's greatest gift to us. We see them on the evening news and encounter them daily. It's all about the people. People challenge one another to grow. Proverbs 27:17 (NIV) states, *"As iron sharpens iron so one man sharpens another."* We make each other better or we make each other weaker by our intended actions or neglect. I find myself equally blessed and disappointed by what I see in the form of people considering other people and how they treat each other.

In the world in which we live, it seems "Every Man for Himself" is the motto. "Me First" is the norm. This breaks my heart and goes against everything I've encountered and learned on how to be successful in this life. How can a person be centered and still be so selfish? I am not talking about being self-centered. Being self-centered is nothing more than selfishness with the world revolving around you and not caring for others.

However, centering yourself allows you to focus on where you want to be and doing what you so desire to accomplish in your life. It allows for you to live your purpose for each season you may be in during your lifetime. Let's face it; most of us have enough failures in our lives, and we don't need anyone reminding us about how inept we are in different areas of our lives. It's like having a constant reminder of failure, and we know it's hard to move forward when we constantly see our failures being put in front of us. I chose to leave people like that behind. I get the accusers out of my life so I can concentrate on the good strengths I have and strengthen my weaker areas. That is how I became centered and the reason I want you to learn to center as well. We are all a work in progress. Not finished until called home. I don't know anyone who has it all, but I do know people, who, like you and I, are working to have all God has for them.

The scripture in Hosea 4:6 (TLB) states, *"My people are destroyed because they don't know me...."* I have heard some scholars interpret that as "My people perish for lack of knowledge." I want people to understand that doesn't mean you just die spiritually and physically and go to heaven. What it means is if you don't get the proper knowledge in every area of your life, then you will experience failure as you watch those areas of your life perish in failure. You can get God's knowledge in all areas of your life. Get the proper knowledge in running your finances so your bank account doesn't perish in bankruptcy. Get the best knowledge you can so your marriage doesn't perish in divorce. Read the Bible and be an active participant with Christ and in a church so your spiritual life doesn't perish. I have failed my way to success in some of these areas, so please take to heart the words I write. I thank God daily that I haven't failed beyond repair. He won't let me when I pay attention and seek His knowledge. Yes, I may fail for a temporary moment in time, but as you will read later in this book, it is just that, temporary.

I'm writing this book with the best of intentions. This book isn't intended to be a literary masterpiece. It is as a manual that is easy to read and reread. It is intended to be used as you are centering yourself to enjoy and master the life you desire. You will see my helpful hints to assist you in remembering key aspects of how centered people live life abundantly. I like what Peter wrote in the book 2 Peter 1:12 (TLB), *"I plan to keep on reminding you of these things even though you already know them and are really getting along quite well!"* There will be things in this book some of you will consider common sense, yet to others will be a new concept. Please read this with an open mind that no matter where we are in our life, we can be reminded to do the right things and do them well.

I'm not finger pointing, nor do I consider myself to have apprehended all knowledge because the Lord knows I have just as much failure as success in being centered and investing in people. However, I have overcome and found success. You may not find things in this book that are exactly new, but the difference is that I will challenge you to live what you know.

I am amazed as I go shopping at the mall or to a sports stadium and I look at the crowds of people and know that Christ loves them all and has a purpose for them all. I am amazed at the number of people in this world. Christ has developed a unique plan for them all. Isn't that amazing? Please open your minds and hearts as we take this little trip together. You may think I am a little weird. I can live with that. Trust me, when I say things haven't always ended up at times like I thought they were going to. That's the fun part of life.

I have friends most people wouldn't give the time of day to. I have friends and acquaintances who are practicing Christianity. Some are practicing homosexuality and lesbianism; some are angry. I have friends who have low self-esteems and bad marriages. I have good friends recovering and restoring their lives as well as friends who have stolen and think nothing is wrong with it. I don't alienate myself from people like a celebrity does. Trust me; I have been tempted to do so at times (after the way I have been treated). However, let me ask you this. If I stay away from people, how will God's love through me ever get to them? They aren't exactly running to church every Sunday. By the look in their eyes at times, I know they are having thoughts, wondering why I would ever give them the time of day. I do because others don't. It's that simple. But you see, I am not like others. I am not embarrassed to know them or identify with them. I will walk in the mall and go to lunch with a friend who is homosexual, only to have his coworkers ask if I am a new boyfriend or something. I have others tease me about it. I don't care what they think of me in their distorted reality. At first when being teased, my pride was a little taken back. But let's face it, that's all it is, a false pride.

I need to make it clear that I don't participate in anyone's sin, but I don't consider myself to be better than they are. I am now just different than they are. I can relate to them because I too am a former practitioner of sin. I was pretty good at it. At times I found my focus on sin instead of on my future. Even as a born again Christian, I could hide my sin pretty well. I was hypocritical. It isn't hypocritical when you are trying to overcome sin that has a stronghold on your life. However, when you point your finger at someone else who is struggling or in sin and act like you are better or are sinless, then you have the problem of being hypocritical. I found I couldn't hide my sin from God, and he made me deal with it. Now I am redeemed and practicing a new way of life.

Therefore, I can embrace people and plant seeds of hope in them. In case you wonder, yes I do share Christ with them. I do tell them what Christ has been doing in my life and why I trust him. It's just like the scripture says to always be of sound mind and ready to give an answer to all who may inquire about my style of life. I am investing in them to bring them to a place of centeredness. I let it be a natural part of our conversation. It doesn't permeate every conversation we have, but they need to see the love that comes from my expressions towards them as much or more than the words that come through my mouth.

Charles Colson, the advisor to former President Nixon and key player in the Watergate scandals, tells audiences that he embraces and physically hugs people who were in prison with him and people who are dying of AIDS. He lets you know he wasn't always comfortable doing that, but he realizes his physical touch is an investment in them of God's love that they may never get in their remaining days alive. He makes a point to do it.

> **h³** HOWARD'S HELPFUL HINT: *Centered people embrace other people.*

I have chosen to take on a service attitude and show you how to invest in yourself and place yourself in a position to invest in others. I will be sharing some of my experiences and failures and what drives me to do this. I am going to impart my passion for this topic on you. I am going to challenge you to question your current and previous ways of thinking as well as challenge you to develop a new mindset that allows you to become a great people investor. That's an investment in yourself and others. Some of these concepts are actually from me and other concepts may look familiar, as others have imparted them to me.

What I am telling you may not be status quo, but it actually comes from my experiences as a healthcare professional, husband, father, friend, athlete, and Christian. I am also including tips I have attained through reading, listening, praying, learning, and observing how to become centered. How many books have you browsed through at the local bookstore only to find that you couldn't relate because it didn't seem practical, logical, or relevant to you? The title is a turn off. The color of the book isn't attractive, and in fact, some of them leave you disappointed with more questions than when you started. Well, hopefully not this one. This book is God-breathed, born of tears, sweat, and joy by someone who actually walked the walk. I am now at a point in my life that I desire to share it with you. I learned that the small experiences of our lives add up to be the direction and vision of who we become in life. You can't be centered and invest in others until you have invested in yourself. So take this book and invest the principles in yourself, and then invest the principles in others.

The Reverend Billy Graham, in an address to the graduating class of Wheaton College in 1993, stated that "God calls us to invest our time capital in the very lives of people-not in projects, not in possessions."[1] He goes on to say, "Time is the capital that God has given us to invest. People are our investment, whether they are blue chips, or penny stocks, or even junk bonds. Jesus was willing to take risks with twelve diverse disciples and he took a great risk with us." He then says "But when we talk of our investment, everyone asks, 'What return will we get?'" He goes on to answer, "A meaningful life that will count for God and fulfillment in our lives." Isn't that a great description of the life God has called us to live? That is what my true heart's desire and calling is. So you now see I have chosen to be towards you, what my Father is towards me.

God himself, the creator of the universe, creator of all you and I can physically and spiritually see, is centered and is a people investor. Look at John 3:16 (NKJV), *"For God so loved the world that he gave his only begotten son that whoever believes in him [Jesus] should not perish but have everlasting life."* In John, Christ brings us full circle in this concept as he states, "That no man can come to the Father except through me." God gave his son so I could have life and have it more abundantly. His son gave his life in obedience to his father as a bond of love that could never be broken. That circle can never be broken. He did it for people, for all mankind including our enemies. That's how much Jesus also loved his father, even unto being the scourge for us on a cross.

So now you know that this is what drives me. *Can I be less?* I am a child of God and all his investment in me. It would be a travesty to never invest in others that life he invested in me. So I decided that *I won't be less!* It is important to tell you that I could have chosen the other way. You may be faced with decisions you haven't made as of yet and you need to. Be brave and make the decision. God isn't going to punish you for moving in faith and perhaps making a wrong decision. He will honor you and continue to love you as you move forward in him. He won't let you fail beyond redemption when you move out in faith. I personally have found that God enjoys seeing us move in faith because it shows how much we trust him.

2

DECIDING TO LIVE A LIFE OF FAITH

I decided a long time ago to live a life of faith. That decision is what has led me to become a centered person. What does living a life of centeredness mean? *To me, it means exercising my beliefs regularly to discover who I am in God and make every possible effort to live that way.* I am centered in my faith, and every other part of my life flows out from that. Even if I can't see the end result or know where it's all heading, I still have to move forward in faith, believing it will all work out for good. I also learn where to make adjustments and not have to be forced to another path because of my own slothfulness or ignorance. Jim Stovall, who congenitally developed blindness during his college years and later developed the Narrative Television network, reminds audiences when he speaks, "Whatever your situation in life, you too, can step out of that safe room and proceed with faith, minute by minute hand over hand, not worrying about what lies ahead or what might happen, but trusting that God will supply you the energy and courage to cope with each experience as it arises." What a remarkable man. I encourage you to read about him in the book *Graduation Moments: Wisdom and Inspiration from the Best Commencement Speakers Ever.* Jim knows better than most that we don't need to have it all figured out before stepping out. Jim struggled with depression and discouragement, just like you and I have. He didn't allow those attacks to stop him from pursuing his God-given vision and desire. That is what faith is. Life requires us to use it. In my life, I have seen God work so many situations for my good just because I stepped out in faith with the right motivation in my heart. But like I mentioned, I had to step out; God didn't push me.

> **h³** HOWARD'S HELPFUL HINT: *Centered people exercise their faith regularly.*

A centered person is a person who is learning to become. It is knowing the person you are and believing in and becoming that person, pursuing by faith, all God has for you. When the person you are meets the person you are becoming, active vibrant change takes place, and you continue to become the centered person God desires you to be. That may sound a little weird, but let's think about it for a moment. You can see who you are currently. You see what you like and don't like and desire to change. So you actually can see the person you are and the person you desire to be simultaneously, that person in you who is developing or, as I like to say, becoming.

What I like about this is that we are never finished until we pass on to be with Christ. II Peter 1:5 (TLB) states, *"...You must also work hard to be good, and even that is not enough. For then you must learn to know God better and better and discover what he wants you to do."* We will discuss "discovering" later in another chapter. My point now is that as you become the centered person you desire, it will be through an exciting process of discovery.

As I mentioned, I still move forward in faith, faith that believes it can and will be better tomorrow than it is today. I used to hear the different denominations such as Baptists,

Methodists, Catholics, and non-denominational churches say they believe things the others don't and interpret Scripture differently from each other. They even have a pride about that at times. I'm okay with that, but it confused the daylights out of me as a young Christian. I kept wondering who was right and who was wrong. That's natural, because I wanted to be right. I didn't want to fail God. So I made a decision. I picked up my Bible and held it up to God and I said, "God I don't understand everything in this book of yours. I don't know whom to believe; so today I declare that I believe you! I believe this isn't a fairytale. I believe you parted the Red Sea and that you led your people and that you continue to lead the people who believe in you. You love people and you care for them, even when they can't care for themselves. I believe you heal people, and I believe your gifts are true even if I never see any of them. I choose to believe in your Word, which is an outpouring of yourself for us." That's the way I live today. I believe that just because I can't physically see heaven or physically see God, still, I have chosen by faith to believe he exists.

Let me ask you, which is easier to say, I believe what I don't see or I believe what I do see? Look at I Peter 1:8 (TLB), *"You love him even though you have never seen him; though not seeing him, you trust him; and even now you are happy with the inexpressible joy that comes from heaven itself."* Verse 9 then states, *"And your further reward for trusting him will be the salvation for your souls."* That's right; I receive eternal life for just trusting God. Many others have gone before us and now cheer us on as we live out our destinies in God. So you see, I'm not taking the easy road here. You are right; it's easier to believe what you see physically. However, in living by faith, you develop senses that believe and see what you can't see with the physical eye, but they are very visible to the spiritual eye. I think most centered people, who are people investors, have this gift.

At times, people look at me and think I'm crazy, but that's because they couldn't live my life of faith. They try to filter it through their own knowledge and experiences. Read that again. Too many times we need a reference point when speaking to people. When we struggle to get one, we then think the other person is a little different in a bad way. Well, the truth is we are all different in a good way. Just because someone is different from us doesn't make him weird. It makes him unique. It makes us unique. How boring would it be if we all were the same as everyone else? I love the uniqueness I see in others—their unique smiles, gifts, kindness, skills, abilities. Think about it for a moment. Don't you miss the uniqueness of a loved one who has passed away? Haven't you noticed that no one can replace the way that person laughed or teased or the friendliness he or she invested? We would be wise to learn from each other's uniqueness instead of judging it because of the differences.

I don't want to make a life of faith sound easy. It is anything but easy, but it's the road less traveled, which means people who live by faith get to see and experience things that those who don't live by faith never get to see and do. Let me give you some simple examples.

I had worked for a hospital system for nineteen years. I was getting bored and restless, so I met with my brother-in-law and had a conversation about it. I felt in my conscience and spirit that God was leading me on. I had a house, a great family, steady job, and great community that I knew like the back of my hand. Yet my spirit desired to live by faith and seek another adventure. It didn't take much faith for me to have those things. It might take others a lot of faith to have those things. I am not being judgmental. I'm relaying my experience. So it took greater faith to move on and leave that past behind so that I could experience and become more than I ever dreamed. One evening, I was eating dinner with my family and I stated my situation to them. I said we would move anywhere but California or New York. I had been both places and had great experiences with great people there but couldn't see me fitting in. I had run the New York City marathon twice, and I thought that the whole state of New York was just like the city. So what happened? That's right; you know God's humor. I got an interview in Syracuse, New York, and when I arrived there, my spirit felt like I was home. So I moved my family there. I didn't just leave the neighborhood in St. Joseph, Missouri. I left the neighborhood, the county, the state, and the region and by faith moved for greater opportunity, risking failure in all areas of my life. Now that took faith, but I know how much bigger God is than me, so it's easier to believe he will help it all work out.

> **h³ HOWARD'S HELPFUL HINT:** *Centered people don't keep looking back or they realize they lose forward momentum.*

I want to mention that moving by faith isn't the same as presumption. I have also done things "presuming" God would make it work out, and when he didn't, I was very disappointed in God and myself. However, my disappointment in and blaming God ended when I realized it was my fault. I realized that I hadn't sought God about it but just presumed it was all okay. I had presumed that God had my back. That's presumption, not faith. Yes, he did protect and love me, and he also grabbed my attention to move in wisdom and not presumption.

It would probably take another book to tell you all the wonderful experiences, wonderful people, and wonderful times my family and I have had in New York. I also shed a lot of tears questioning if it was the right thing for my family and me to have made such a major move at that time in our lives. Had

I caused them pain by leaving their friends and the life they knew? Yes, I did. But to this day, they will tell you it was worth it because of the experiences and the people they met and the blessings received. Was it easy? No. It was far from it. Was it worth the price paid? Yes! We couldn't have bought the experiences we have had if we had stayed in our comfort zone.

> h³ HOWARD'S HELPFUL HINT: *Centered people get out of their comfort zone to experience unique success.*

People said I was crazy; I would be back in Missouri in a year. Even the people in New York said that. No one was cutting me any slack and most weren't encouraging me to move. Most didn't welcome me in the move. I felt the Lord impress upon me that, even though people doubted me and talked about me behind my back, he was preparing a table for me in the presence of my enemies. I understood my enemies were not flesh and blood. The unseen forces spiritually didn't want me to succeed and tried everything they could to discourage me, and they ultimately failed. The move appeared to be a mountain I wasn't going to be able to accomplish. But six years later, I'm still in New York experiencing God's goodness and blessings and sharing with others. I would never have chosen this without a vision and encouragement from God that this was the right thing to do. I had allowed bad experiences and prejudices to cloud my thinking and almost made a decision to quit. I thank God that he desired so much more for me than I could have imagined, and he gave me the faith to step out and explore it. Let me give you another example.

Your life is like a mountain. You can probably climb most of the mountain alone without much assistance, or at least with minimal assistance. Then one day, you look up at the mountain, see the summit, and realize that you will never get there alone. The mountain is so large and at times treacherous. You realize you will need new tools, plans, and attributes if you are going to make it to the top. Clouds hide the peak, and some days you can't even see the peak as it is hidden behind weather and the storms of life. You know the peak is still there waiting for you to conquer it, but because today's challenges are all you can handle. You don't even allow yourself to believe you could reach it. You may get discouraged and never look up at it again. You don't want to see what you can't have. It is too painful and discouraging to realize a dream may have just been lost.

> **h³** HOWARD'S HELPFUL HINT: *Centered people know they were never intended to climb the mountains of life alone.*

Well, now you can relax. God never intended for us to walk this life alone. We are all part of a body of the human race. We all contribute differently. There are people you know or whom you will be introduced to at a time you really need them. You are interconnected with many people you don't even know and haven't met yet. These people are God's gift to help you reach the peak and summits of your mountains in life. Don't take them for granted. Let them contribute to you and you contribute to them. You will reach your peak. Also understand that the peak looks different when you reach it than when you were standing at the bottom of the mountain looking up at it. I have ridden horses on some of Colorado's most beautiful mountains. I was shocked to learn a horse could navigate the steepness and narrowness of the paths. I was also surprised at the gorgeous marshes hidden on the mountains. I witnessed some of the most beautiful wildlife and natural habitat imaginable. I wouldn't have been able to do this sitting still and just looking up and marveling at the size of the mountains. I got to see things that only those who dared to climb would ever get to see. These places on the mountain are hidden from the naked eye when you are at the bottom. I had to actively make an effort to challenge the hills and narrow paths and heights. I had to place my trust in an animal I didn't know and a guide I had just barely met. But, oh, what a beautiful journey it turned out to be. I was thankful I had paid the price and had the courage to climb it.

Your life is like that mountain. The centered life you desire can be yours. It may seem scary at times. It may appear impossible. You may not think you can make your way to the top. That's usually when God gets to show his faithfulness to you and show you what he can do through you. He will do things through you that you believed were impossible before you actually accomplished them. After that, it will come easier for you as your confidence grows with each new success. You can't live a centered life sitting there looking up at it. You have to approach it in faith.

Since moving to New York, I have prayed with and counseled people whom others would not give any attention. I would never have even met these people if I had chosen to play it safe in Missouri. That showed me that God allowed my moving to New York to be a blessing to them as well. That's how much God loves others. The move was so much bigger than me. God used it to allow me to invest in others and become more than I thought possible. How about that? God loves people so much more than we fathom that he sends a man from Missouri to New York to invest love in people in their times of need. I want to say also that those people have been a blessing to me in a big way. It was a two-way street of blessing for me. I was living in New York when what we now call 9/11 happened, and therefore, I helped to prepare a hospital to receive wounded patients. There's no arrogance in the statements I have just made. God isn't using me to save the world. That's his job. But by moving in faith, he is allowing me to make a difference in my spheres of influence.

I have met politicians on the highest level. Yes, the president and congressmen, national champion baseball, basketball, football, golf, lacrosse, and many other sports professionals. I have visited almost all major sports halls of fame. I have visited West Point and the Military Museum and marveled at the odds our forefathers overcame. I have marveled at the people and what they accomplished, oftentimes against many odds. I have learned much by observing these people in action. I have met numerous authors including, Andy Rooney of televisions 60 Minutes; Senator and former First Lady, Hilary Rodham Clinton; John Miller, author of *The Question behind the Question;* and many others. I have met many famous musicians and entertainers, including my favorite The Trans-Siberian Orchestra. I have been to the Eagles Nest in Germany, the famous hideout of Hitler. I have been to FDR's library and heard his famous D-Day speech. I have visited the Lincoln Memorial in Washington DC—just to mention a few. I have done so much more but I can save that for another point. Why did I do these things? I am not telling you this to impress you. I have had a desire to contribute to a nation of people just like these people have. These were all people anointed and called to do more for something other than themselves. Some abused their positions while the centered people flourished in it. They did this at many times through great sacrifice and personal pain.

I like the scripture in Psalms 16: 3 (TLB) that states, *"I want the company of the Godly men and women in the land; they are the true nobility."* People who have a godly focus know how to treat and enjoy people and serve people. Of course, Hitler isn't a hero of anyone who has a sound mind. However, I learned much about visiting WWII historical places, as well as others. I was totally taken aback by man's inhumanity to man. But then I developed a greater understanding of how man could have scourged Christ. I was proud to see what our forefathers did to overcome his demonic regimes. It is different when you actually see it instead of just reading about it. At times, these people were called to accomplish things they wouldn't have wished upon other people including their enemies. I admired the fact that they did not shrink back but moved forward and performed in passion that which no other was called to do or could have done the way they did.

> **h³** HOWARD'S HELPFUL HINT: *In order to succeed, centered people do the hard things and do them right.*

These people accepted the responsibility given to their position in life. I also understand and admire that these great people failed. Do you ever wonder who actually confirmed these were great people? I think we do, when we realize we can relate to people who overcome great odds and challenges and come out the other side changed and stronger and still contributing.

Yes, these people have had both personal and professional failures in their lives. However, they never let their personal or professional failures define them or stop them. What I did find is that they too move in faith to make things better and to invest in others. I would like to point out, however, that having met them doesn't mean that those are among my proudest moments. I don't need to brag about meeting anyone. It doesn't make me feel important because I have rubbed elbows with the famous. I have people closer to me that I admire more, and that many of you will never know because they aren't famous. Just because they aren't famous doesn't mean they are less in God's eyes. My proudest precious moments with them are hidden deeply in my heart for only me. The people I have mentioned, just to name a few, are people God allowed me to come in contact with and see that they aren't so different from you and I, other than they have made choices most wouldn't make in faith. They used their innate passion for what they do and what they desired to accomplish and what they believed they were called to accomplish. By moving in faith, they allowed what they were called to do to unfold in front of them.

h³ HOWARD'S HELPFUL HINT: *Centered and successful people make decisions others aren't willing to make.*

They place themselves in the game. They go where the game is being played, and they enter the stadium to compete in it. You can't do that sitting still and being self-centered. You do that by being centered. Now doesn't that just make the hair on your neck stand up and give you chills? To think you could be the same person and do great things like these people did?

Most people have a desire but don't translate that into a passion. To reach your dreams and live by faith, you have to have the fire of that passion burning in you. I mean it has to burn so you feel it and can't do anything but work towards it. I don't want to make it sound like everyone has to do some national or statewide accomplishment or that they are a failure if they didn't reach their passion.

Read the story of Samuel in the Bible—how Samuel's mother's desire was to have a child to raise and give him to the service of the Lord. Wow! Her investment in that child was so important that we still read about it thousands of years later. That child helped give God's prophetic voice to a struggling nation of people. I'm sure it wasn't so glamorous when she was changing diapers and cooking. However, her dream and passion was realized. She performed her passion in private. A nation reaped the benefit. King David was led to repentance through this man of God and kept his soul from hell.

This book you are reading is for men and women alike. Please hear what I'm writing and let it challenge and inspire you. When I was married for about ten years, I would toss and turn in my bed when I was supposed to be sleeping. My wife would ask me what was wrong. I would answer her by saying, "I don't know except that I feel I'm supposed to do something great, and I'm not doing anything to reach whatever it is I'm supposed to be doing." I don't mean that I'm supposed to fly to the moon. But God had placed a passion in my spirit to live by faith and accomplish and experience much more than I was allowing him to work through me. My critics would say that it was just my Type A personality needing to conquer another passion. Perhaps. However, if that is what God placed in my spirit to inspire and move me, then so be it. From then on I quit sitting still, and I have grabbed this passion with all my might. I will not quit until I'm called home. One last thing about this— if it cost me my family because I didn't pay enough attention to them during this, then I would consider that a major failure. Those close to me should be able to pick up most easily from me, the concepts I am sharing with you. My whole life wouldn't be a failure, but to have an area where my family failed under my watch would be a hard personal pain for me to overcome. Although, I may point out that many great men and women of God have experienced this type of failure and still have been great contributors to our society.

> h³ Howard's Helpful Hint: *Centered people have two common threads to their success— humility and perseverance.*

I have had the opportunity to watch firsthand many successful coaches on all levels of sports. I agree with what I heard Mike Krzyzewski of Duke University say once during an interview. He said that there are better coaches than he, coaching in division three and other levels. He acknowledged he was fortunate to be where he was and given the opportunities to do what he did. He understood the price he had to pay and therefore appreciated the humbleness that was worked through him through the fires of life. I have taken the opportunity to watch firsthand three successful basketball coaches. Two won national NCAA championships, and one led our Olympic team in Sydney to a gold medal. I observed Gino Auriemma of UCONN, who has five National championships, Muffet McGraw the longtime Notre Dame head coach won the 2001 national championship, and Nell Fortner of Olympic Championship and ESPN and coaching her new team at Auburn University. All of these coached games in Syracuse. I would get a ticket and sit directly behind their bench and listen and observe as they coached and motivated their teams to victory. I noticed how they all surrounded themselves with successful people, who in turn assist in helping their teams be successful. I would look in their eyes and notice the intensity and passion with which they looked at their players. I listened to their voices as they raised and lowered them in response to the situations. I listened to the words they used in getting players attention and motivating players. I observed as they knew what buttons to push to get the response necessary from their team. I observed their approach to the game. They understand in the scope of life it is "just a game." They all kept their emotions in check, even under some intense pressure. They didn't blame others, like the referees, for any of their failures. I read their personal profiles on their team websites and learned they work hard and have come from humble beginnings. They also had others go before them and invest in them what they have learned so they could in turn pass it on to future generations. They also know that the investment they are making in their players and staff is more than a game. They were preparing players and assistant coaches in becoming people of character to carry on and be successful on their own when new opportunities arose.

I watched as Nell Fortner led her Auburn University women's basketball team to a victory. Late in the second half, she gathered her players around during a timeout and listened to what they had to say and smiled as they spoke, all the while looking into their eyes. It was obvious the players weren't playing up to Nell's standards, however she knew what they needed from her and she was confident that her players would eventually get from her the message she was communicating. After each timeout, they would yell in unison "Togetherness." That reminded me of Christ's command to us to love our neighbor as ourselves. To want for others what you desire for yourself. Nell was teaching her first year players to look out for each other and have each other's best interest in mind while on the court. She didn't allow them to play an individual game unless it was part of the team's success. It has been said that all of these coaches have an infectious personality. In other words, they attract good people and success. This isn't only because of who they are but because people close to them understand their passion for what they do as well as their passion for those they do it with. These are true people investors. This makes people like them attractive to us all.

There are many more people in life one can observe for the success you are looking for. I have witnessed successful teachers, pastors, public servants, nurses, paramedics, trainers, police officers, and many others from whom many lessons of success can be learned. I don't want you to read this and think that coaches are the only ones from whom you can learn. There are many people close to you from whom you can observe these lessons to invest in others if you are willing to observe.

3

WHAT KIND OF CENTERED PERSON DO YOU WANT TO BECOME?

Centered people ask themselves: *what kind of centered person do I want to become?* Have you ever asked yourself that question? How can I ask that when I don't even know who I am? Are you the type that goes along with the status quo—not rocking the boat because of what others may think? Have you become what others wanted you to be and not what you really desired to be? Have you allowed past hurts to stop you in your tracks and not chase your dream? It's not too late; I don't care how old you are. It's easier than you may realize. You can determine through your choices the kind of person you want to be. In Proverbs 19:22 (TLB) its states, "kindness makes a man attractive." Do you know anyone who wants to be around mean, unkind people? Are you attracted to that sort of person? If so, then check your heart and see why and get help. The flip side is that unkindness makes a man or woman unattractive. I don't want to be around those types of people. I am not fun to be around when I'm not kind. That may sound simple, but that's part of deciding who it is you want to become. I see people coming to work who just don't want to be there, and they don't care who knows it. They can't leave their baggage at the door. They have to bring it in with them for everyone else to trip over. Perhaps that's you.

Then let's change your direction and go after what you desire to be. Think of people you admire. What qualities stand out to you about them? Are they kind, strong, wealthy, educated, loving, givers not takers, and have close family? Are they risk takers? Do they place others before themselves? You can develop those qualities as well.

I know of one extremely successful author and speaker who hired a coach because he realized he wasn't, in his own words, "likeable." He was intelligent, had money and a beautiful family, was an asset to his community, yet to become successful as a speaker, he had to find a way to become likeable. His demeanor didn't attract people the way he wanted it to, so he became who he wanted to be by recognizing and overcoming who he was. He developed the necessary skills to make the changes to overcome his shortcomings. He hired a personal coach to help him become likeable. How cool is that? Now he has several published books and has a successful keynote speaking tour of approximately seventy dates a year. He has even been a keynote speaker and shared the same stage and night as Lou Holtz, the famous football coach. People who aren't likeable don't get those types of opportunities. We all have that ability and choice to make. Proverbs 19:20 (TLB), *"Get all the advice you can and be wise for the rest of your life."*

I know you have heard it said, "it is not where you start but where you finish that counts." That is so true. This journey you are on will end in success as you make choices, implement centeredness, and decide who it is you want to become.

> **h³** HOWARD'S HELPFUL HINT: *Centered people learn to "become."*

As people who are centered, we realize that in life we are becoming. At times we have to go after life. At other times it seems life just comes to us with little effort. I find those latter times rare.

In my travels, I have failed to find the perfect mentor or coach. Are they out there? Of course they are. Just look on the World Wide Web and find coaches who are willing for a fee to coach you. What I'm getting at is the fact that I have to run to them for help. They aren't running to help me. Before any of my friends read this and become offended, I have to say I have friends and colleagues who have invested in my life and that's certainly a major reason why I am where I am today. You and I have both good and bad because of investments made and deposited in us. I have my spouse, children, teachers, CEOs, football coaches, pastors, friends, and colleagues who have all invested in me to make me successful. I find that I am mentored more by what I observe than what people directly tell me. To them I owe myself to make sure I am in turn reinvesting their deposits in you as well. We all have people who inspired us and made us want to be better than we are. That inspiration can come in the form of children, adults, adolescents, middle-aged, and the elderly. You have to look for it and be open to it.

> HOWARD'S HELPFUL HINT: *Centered people have developed openness about themselves.*

You have to place yourself in a position to receive it. You have to open yourself up to receive these people. You have to decide to be a person who is teachable. By reading this book, that's exactly what you are doing. You are learning to process and become an investor in yourself so that others can benefit from your experiences and who you have become. I had another well-published author tell me the thing that makes him angry is when someone asks him, "How do you find time to write?" This author has published several novels and sold the movie rights as well. He had fire in his eyes when he shared that with me. I could tell it was a main irritant to him, and I was equally happy I wasn't the one who asked it. I laughed and told him to ask them, "When do you find time to watch TV?" He laughed at my retort. I got his message. He was telling me those people with passion will be the ones to pay the price to do what it takes to *become* who they really desire to be.

h³   HOWARD'S HELPFUL HINT: *Centered people learn to impart.*

I have seen and heard this topic of centeredness delivered in different forms. However, I've never seen it spoken or delivered like I'm speaking to you now. You ask, "How can you be speaking to me? After all, I'm reading this book." As you are reading, these words get in your mind and spirit by me imparting them to you. The anointing on me to write this is imparted to you, as it would be by any good writer and author. You feel a connection as you read. You agree that this book is just what you need for this time in your life. That's the anointing you feel. It's an anointing to meet your specific need in a specific place and time. This isn't just another book on leadership or how to or self-help. This is a quick manual for you to read and study. It isn't Albert Einstein's theory of relativity. It isn't that difficult or revealing. For you to be successful, you must meditate on the concepts and allow God to expand on the helpful hints I give. Then, prioritize them and take action. After reading this, you won't be the same person. If you put the concepts in place and use them as tools to help you, you can become all you have desired and dreamed of. You will have to do the work. I am just giving you the tools necessary to impart and plant spiritually and mentally in you to help you grow.

> **h³**   HOWARD'S HELPFUL HINT: *Centered people are unashamed to be called a servant.*

Centered people serve others. Matthew 23:11 (NKJV) says, *"But he who is greatest among you shall be your servant."* Do you desire to be the greatest? Then serve people. I am not ashamed to be called a servant. Being a servant is an attitude of choice. Being a servant isn't being a slave. I think a lot of times people unknowingly confuse the two concepts. There is freedom in serving; there is only bondage in slavery. One is a choice; the other isn't. Being a servant is not a demeaning title or role. According to the Bible, it is the greatest role and attitude a person could actually take on and become. Who, by knowing that, would not want to become a servant? Knowing what I just described, who fits that picture in your life? You know, the actual creator of the universe serves us by answering our prayers. I doubt he is sitting on the throne worried if someone thinks less of him because he serves us lowly humans.

As an example, the one obvious person to me is a mother. Mothers seem to be the best at having a servant's heart. Look at what they invest in us. Howard's five "L's": Love, Laundry, Lunch, Lessons, and Life. It just doesn't get much better than that. I will also add it's a very hard and time-consuming role. Just ask your mom. But I bet she would tell you that the investment she made in you was well worth the price of serving you the five L's. To be a servant is to focus at times on another person instead of yourself, and at times, it doesn't seem very rewarding. That's because you can't always see the results

EXCEL AT LIVING A CENTERED LIFE 45

instantly. But trust me, you will eventually see them. Perhaps your mother saw you as you are today and not still as the five-year-old she had to clean up after. Women oftentimes don't get the credit they deserve for the hard work they lovingly invest in their families. That's how being centered enables you to endure the hardships until the end. You can see the dream before it is ever fully manifested.

When you're planting the seeds of investment in yourself and others, just water it and let it grow on its own. The results depend on the stewardship others take from what you invest in them and the stewardship you place in what you invest in yourself. The result can't be guaranteed unless those who receive the investment will pay the price to grow to success. As you read this book, make a decision to invest in yourself so you can invest in others.

Personally speaking, I wished and dreamed of having a person invest in me the way I invest in others. Perhaps it may be unrealistic to expect such a thing. I haven't actually found that one person, but I have found others and taken it upon myself to go after them and their wisdom. If they won't come to me, I will go to them. It beats sitting around in self-pity doesn't it? I take an active role in my life instead of a passive role. An active or passive role, either one you choose, is still a role. Choose wisely.

This book contains the wisdom I have personally experienced and those that some other people investors have invested in me and written in other books to help us believe and achieve. Grab the investment and run.

4

Who Helped Center You?

For a moment, think of the people you have met and the books you have read, the movies you have watched, the teachers who taught you, the coaches who coached you, the parents, pastors, priests who prayed for you and imparted to you. What is the one characteristic that you instantly notice? I find it to be love. A second one is time, their time. They all loved to impart to people and give of themselves to make you better and help you. After thinking of them, what do you remember? What stood out in your mind about them? Did you find yourself smiling, crying, and laughing as you remembered them? What response did their thoughts elicit from you? That's what they invested in you. Make a decision to be a steward of their investment. Be just as serious about that investment as if they deposited money in the bank and you are responsible to make it grow with an interest rate. They cared enough for you, now you care enough to steward and grow and give them a return on their investment. They thought you were worth investing in. So do I. I haven't met half the people who may read this book. Since others thought you were worth the investment, please give me the privilege of investing in you as well. If our paths cross, I am also hoping you will give me a return on this investment by showing me and telling me what you have learned from this.

What's an investor? It's a person who takes something they consider valuable and places it in a process that will give them a return of growth as they steward it. Read that line again. What do you hope to have happen when you invest? You want a return. You want growth, more, plenty, abundance! Remember, you also have to be a faithful steward with it. You can't just invest it and never look at it again. That's what I'm after with you as well. To invest enough in you that you have the tools and growth to be abundantly more than where you started out to be. Let's get started!

> **h³** HOWARD'S HELPFUL HINT: *Centered people live a life of discovery.*

Early in life, I discovered the hardest person in the world to know was myself. I find that humorous considering all the time I spend with me. I look in the mirror at me. I sleep with me. I eat with me. I dress me. Heck, I even talk to me. Some of my best conversations are with myself (laughing). Yet still, I found it hard to know who I was, where I was going, what I really wanted to do in life, and what I was placed on this earth to do and become. I find we all struggle through that discovery. I finally gave in and decided to be the person I had become and was becoming and not try to be someone else. But, to "be comfortable in my own skin" wasn't easy, and it has taken me many years. I quit thinking and caring what others thought of me and what others wanted me to be. That was my conflict. I was a people pleaser. So to be and please others didn't fit where I was going in my heart. I would want to be like some rock star or NFL Player or someone I admired. The television and others were constantly telling us how important these people were and insinuating to us that we weren't as important. I had allowed that to make me feel inadequate. One day God said, *"You know, Howard, I already have rock stars and football players. I want one of you."* He was impressing upon me that I wasn't a failure, but that I needed to discover who it was he wanted me to become in him. God didn't need me to be an imitator of someone else. He wanted me to discover in him who I was genuinely supposed to be.

> **h³** HOWARD'S HELPFUL HINT: *God wants one like you too. Go for it!*

I knew other people. I could see their talents, their good looks, and their dreams as they shared them. I witnessed how others had favored them above me. But as life went on, I questioned if I really knew them. I found that I didn't really know them and chances are they didn't really know themselves either. Most of us don't because we are evolving and growing and becoming and pursuing, and chances are one, two, five, and even ten years from now, we will have the same core values. But we will have grown far beyond being that uncertain young person we have been. I am not the same person I was at eighteen (thank God), nor am I the same person I was at twenty-seven. Like a student, I am still studying life itself as I take my journey. I am still growing and evolving into the person I was intended to be. How do I know that? Because being centered feels right and manifests itself in ways that centers me and allows me to invest in others' lives.

> **h³** HOWARD'S HELPFUL HINT: *Centered people are students of life and for life.*

That's what I love about life. Every day is a new day with a new morning. It's a chance to put the past behind and still strive ahead to be more, give more, love more, invest more, see more, and forgive more. I get to see one more person, one more sunrise, one more sunset, and one more child. I *get* to become more. I don't *have* to become more. I *get* to! My failures can be put behind me, and I can strive toward living a fun life with my direction corrected in the Lord.

Discovery involves seeking and learning and bravely opening new doors, new horizons, and new beginnings. I was watching the movie *Hook,* starring Robin Williams as Peter Pan. In the movie, his old friends recognized him as who we was even though he had physically changed. However, he had blocked any memory of his past because it was too painful to look back. Then Tinker Bell stated, "Yeah it's you. You are the Pan."

He responded asking her, "How do you know?"

Tinker stated, "Because you have the smell of someone who has ridden the backs of the wind." That was my favorite part of the movie. That inspired me. I always struggled to put into words what I was feeling or desiring. I wanted to be like the person who rode the backs of the wind, always having and experiencing adventures. Is that you? Do you want to ride the backs of the wind? Do you have a desire to center yourself so that others recognize you as having made a significant contribution to the world? It may require you to sacrifice and give up a certain lifestyle of comfort. But let me assure you; you won't regret it.

5

How Do I Discover?

How do I know what to discover and how to become centered since I don't know what questions to ask? Okay, let's discover the questions to ask. It's not always the questions you need to ask. It is also just taking an introspective look to who you are now and expanding on that. I will show you as we look at the seven areas of your life to develop later in the book.

Robert Schuller encourages in his book *Tough Times Don't Last but Tough People Do*. This is one I truly love and use with my management teams in building businesses and setting vision. He makes you consider the tough questions. I have heard others, like Tony Robbins, ask things as well. He asks, "If you could do one thing in life and be guaranteed success, you couldn't fail, and finances weren't an issue—what would it be?"

You see the answer to that question reveals our deepest desires. If answered honestly, most of us would answer with words that would describe something much larger than we currently are, something that makes us smile, and makes us want to go for it, something to share with people and have fun doing. That is the thing you are probably supposed to become, at least for now.

I love what Schuller encourages next. After he asks the question, he says, "Now go do it." My first reaction, which probably

EXCEL AT LIVING A CENTERED LIFE 51

wasn't a new reaction, was: what? Go do it? Are you crazy? I might fail! No, I will fail. It's probably a fantasy anyway. People will laugh! I don't have the faith for it. I certainly don't have the finances for it! My spouse will think I'm nuts. I might think I'm nuts! So? Let's say all that is true. Am I going to quit now or take the challenge and do what's necessary to accomplish it?

Remember the movie *Field of Dreams?* Kevin Costner kept hearing a voice telling him, "Ease their pain." He was questioning who and what pain? All he knew was he had to finish the project and see it to the end to get his answers. All the people in the community thought he was crazy. He didn't care what they thought and persevered to get his answer. He didn't let embarrassment or fear of failure get in his way. Then he received an answer he never expected. He learned that it was also his pain that needed relieving. That strong desire God planted in your heart many years ago needs to be released and manifested through you. Do you have a similar pain that needs relieving? It can't be manifested through anyone else. Only you can say it and deliver the way you can. You aren't a pretender. The only imitator you are is of those who, by faith, moved out and contributed their calling to the world. I hope you are inspired to do so. I want you to. I may even be blessed by what you have to share with us. Please accept the challenge.

The easy thing to do now is to sit in self-pity and quit and think that dream is for someone else. You may think that you couldn't possibly do that. Really? Are you content being in a self-pity pouter and partier mode, fearful to attempt and risk living and discovering a dream, even at the expense of failure? I don't think so. You may experience a little of that fear and doubt for a time, but don't let it stop you. Don't look at what you currently have or where you are or reasons you can't move forward.

h³   HOWARD'S HELPFUL HINT: *Start imagining*
what it will be like when you succeed
instead of what it will be like if you fail.

I will write this several times in this book, *centered peo-*
ple give themselves permission to succeed and permission to fail. It
will be okay. It hasn't stopped people who have had dreams of
running for public and private offices or school boards. Think
about it for a second, do you really think any less of a person
who was not elected to a position? Every election, we see someone's dream or desire end, or as I like to think, just take another
direction. I don't think any less of them either. They dared to
try, and I love the Teddy Roosevelt speech from 1910 when he
stated, "It's not the critic who counts, the credit belongs to
the man who is actually in the arena, whose face is marred by
dust and sweat and blood. The man who dared to step into
the arena and give all he had to give. Not the timid soul who
knew nothing of winning and defeat." I know this was written
in 1910, but ladies it applies to you as well. Today, many women
are also realizing their God-given desires to be all that God
has desired for them to be and are making valuable local and
national contributions.

6

LET THE JOURNEY BEGIN

Well now that you are in a total state of shock, let the journey of discovery and becoming begin. You are now going on an adventure to discover who you are, what you desire, what you will be investing in to make yourself and others' lives better and your opportunity to leave the world better than you found it. Most of us fail, in that we make a decision to not do what it takes to make the next steps. I speak from experience. I have worked with professional coaches who know how important this phase of discovery is. They know that if you don't keep discovering, then you tend to take with you the same habits, problems, tendencies, and unrealized potential that you have always let lie dormant. They have programs and easy question tests that allow you to discover your personality tendencies and exercises that allow you to discover your values. Most are scientifically based, and I have found them useful. However, I still go back to say that no matter what you learn and no matter what input a coach and others give you, you still have to follow your heart and internal desires. There will be a peace in it, even though there are still unanswered questions. These tests just help you to discover. I find sometimes they help me clarify the thing I was having trouble expressing. You can't flunk it, so don't be afraid to take one. Your spirit and conscience will let you know if that really isn't you or if it's what you actually desire. It takes faith and courage to follow through with that new found knowledge but it pays off if you follow the journey and the road less traveled.

7

FROM DROPOUT TO SUCCESS

I'm a high school dropout. Now before you throw this book away, just give me a little more time to explain and invest in you. Remember when I said I was glad I wasn't the same person I was at eighteen or even twenty-seven? That's because on my seventeenth birthday, I dropped out of high school and enlisted in the army. At eighteen, I was completing a GED. At nineteen, I was being sent to Germany to serve our country. At twenty-seven, I was graduating with a diploma in nursing. At thirty, I was graduating with a BSN in nursing. At thirty-six, I was graduating from the University of Missouri School of Medicine with a master's degree in healthcare administration. At forty-five, I had completed five years of hospital administration at a level one university teaching hospital, the highest level in the world of health care as we know it. My spouse was finishing her master's degree at Syracuse University. My daughter was in college on a scholarship, and my son was a senior in high school on successful football and wrestling teams, discovering who he wanted to be.

Today, I'm going from being a writer to becoming an author. So you see, I learned to be a centered person, and I have invested in myself and others and others invested in me as well to become more than I dreamed I could be as that seventeen-year-old lost young man. If I had seen that timeline at my young age, I would have messed it up because I wouldn't have been able to believe I could have become the person I now am. Yet, I am not content being the person I now am. As you center and find that life is a journey, you too will yearn for more in a self-actualized way. Now, hopefully I have convinced you to stay along for the ride.

---

h³ HOWARD'S HELPFUL HINT: *Centered people aren't afraid to ask questions.*

As pointed out earlier, I find the questions often are just as important as the answers. It's the questions that lead us in the direction and the answers just confirm that's where we believe we should be going, or assist us in changing directions. I used to have people tell me how weak it was to ask questions. Well, guess what? "Einstein's" asking questions is what moves us along and energizes us to delve deeper into life. What if Eddison had quit at developing the light bulb filament at the 1999th time he tried and failed? But on the 2000th try he was successful. I wonder what he learned on that last try that made him successful. I wonder how he felt, tired, exhausted, and exhilarated? That wouldn't be an uncommon response after finishing a race. Where would we be if NASA hadn't asked questions about space? You realize some of the computer technology developed by NASA is used in our home computers today. They pushed the envelope so to speak, and civilization as a whole benefited. I desire that you do the same pushing in an honorable and respectful and healthy way. *Asking questions isn't a sign of weakness, but a sign of security.* I'm secure enough to ask questions I already know the answer to just to see if you can offer me another perspective on it. Remember, you and I are students of life and learning. That's how we learn and discover. Let others be too intimidated to ask or ashamed they may be laughed at. Not you. You keep asking. You keep pushing forward. You determine above all else that you are going to get yours.

> **h³** HOWARD'S HELPFUL HINT: *Centered people develop purpose.*

Centered people have a purpose. Sometimes their purpose and passion melt into one. Look again at NFL quarterbacks. They love the game with a passion and pour themselves into it. They study when we are out playing. They work behind the scenes so they don't fail in front of everyone. Every game they play is an opportunity to succeed and to fail. I might add that just because they lost on the scoreboard, doesn't necessarily mean they failed. Developing a purpose requires knowing what direction you are heading. When you answer the purpose and direction question, you then need to develop the following discipline. How do I know what my purpose in life is? Here is a simple way to begin. Start by asking what is your heart's desire? Then make that desire your purpose. Sound too simple? It's not, and I don't want to make it sound too easy. I also believe it changes with the seasons of our lives.

> **h³** HOWARD'S HELPFUL HINT: *Centered people realize that we have to keep recreating*

Recreating is what keeps us fresh and vibrant. Women who are mothers experience this. When their children are young, they take up almost all of the mother's time. Then when the seasons of life change and the children grow older and self-sufficient, the mother's role changes from one of caregiver to one of mostly support. The role of mother isn't what it used to be, and now she must recreate herself. She may decide to go back to college and finish a degree or get a job or travel. She has learned to recreate herself. Hopefully, she recreates herself with whatever her passion truly is. If your desire or passion is to pastor a church, then go meet with active vibrant pastors and ask them to help you learn to pursue this knowledge and passion. If it is to write a book, then pursue local authors and ask them for input, but more importantly begin to write. Perhaps you desire to be a successful small business owner, then find some successful small business owners and talk to the local chamber of commerce to make connections. I will guarantee you they are more than happy to talk to you about becoming successful.

8

CENTERED PEOPLE EAT THEIR FOOD:
A FOUR COURSE MEAL

I love to create. I love to create new ideas and new feelings of hope and optimism. So it comes as no surprise I like to create acronyms. Anyone that knows me knows I love acronyms. Acronyms help me to remember what it takes to be successful. Let me share one I developed that keeps me centered, and I invest it in my management teams and others to whom I give personal coaching. It's called *"Food." Food* helps me stay on course. Get it, "course?" Okay, that was just a grinner not a laugher. However, I haven't met a centered person who didn't develop these skills.

Food stands for Focus, Order, Organization, and Diligence. I also add another D for dessert, which stands for Discipline. Let's take each of these, and let me show you what they are and how investing these in your life and others will cause a faster growth.

Centered People Develop Focus

One cannot underestimate the power of focus. Just look at world champion athletes to catch a glimpse of focus. Look at racecar drivers. Look at moms, dads, and scientists. To be focused means to have no distractions. You have learned or are learning to eliminate the distractions that are taking away from you and not contributing towards your goal or vision in life. Does television add to your focus? If the answer is no, then learn to discipline yourself from its unfocused time. When you watch television, all you are seeing is what others desire for you to see. Take control and see what you desire. How many marathon runners do you see sitting at home using the Internet eight hours a day? Probably none if they are successful. They understand that focus causes them to become the runner they desire to be. I have found men and women who have accomplished what we believe to be unthinkable because they pushed the limits further than they ever believed possible. They pushed it when their bodies said, "I quit," but their minds said "No way! I won't quit." I read an article in GQ where a man ran 220 miles by running for three days. He stated he woke up at times in the middle of the road and would get up and keep running. He said he ran while sleeping. He carried a cell phone and ordered pizza so he could eat and accomplish his goal of seeing how far he could push his body. How amazing![2]

On other fronts, what would happen if in a war the troops lost focus? Disaster, certain defeat, and tragedy. I have seen leaders constantly questioned and second-guessed in wartime and times of trying to move an institution forward. But instead of losing focus, they developed strategies that helped them answer the critics and maintain poise and accomplish the goal and vision they set out to do. It's done by focus. It is so important to develop skills that allow you to overcome your weaknesses. You do this first and foremost by controlling your mind and emotions.

I played in football and basketball games where calls went against us and so did many other things. At a young age, I learned to focus and not hear the crowd or let the calls affect me. I realized it didn't matter; I was still in the game and still had to give 100 percent so our team could win. We all have critics and distractions. Those who decide to overcome them are the ones who realize their full potential. At the very least, learn to minimize your weaknesses. I have even changed my language from calling those areas weaknesses to referring to them as opportunities for growth. In reality, that is what they are.

Centered People Develop Order

Order is a tool that one needs to develop to keep his focus on track. Order reminds you to be and stay focused and move in a calculated direction daily and consistently. Order gives direction to how you are going to perform daily in accomplishing your vision. Remember to not forget these are not passive ideas I'm telling you. They are deliberate and calculated actions requiring much effort. It won't happen because you have a vision, but it will happen because you use order like a tool to stay on course.

Centered People Develop Organization

How many times have we moved forward without being organized? What does that do to you? Do you remember how you felt in front of others when your thoughts and dreams and words were unorganized as you spoke? How do we expect our vision to be realized if it's unorganized? Regardless of how much you express it, no one else will be able to see an unorganized vision. Even you won't be able to see your vision as clearly if it is unorganized. Parts of it appear missing. When you see it, it appears like a jigsaw puzzle with the pieces missing. It paints a confusing picture. Be organized and watch the pieces fall together and success rapidly approach. Having organization as a tool in your approach allows the employees in your organization to catch your vision and understand the mission.

Centered People Develop Diligence

Diligence is being constantly consistent. Keep doing the right things at the right time in the right way and the right result will happen. It has been said that to keep doing the same thing and expect different results is a form of insanity. For instance, to keep eating desserts when you are trying to lose weight could be a form of that. You can't lose weight while eating deserts. So then the habits have to change. They will, if you add diligence to your daily routines. If we keep spending and hiring without diligently keeping our hands on the financial aspects of an organization, we will fail. Something always gives when we are diligent. That obstacle that seemed to be impossible to remove was overcome by our diligence.

Centered People Develop Discipline

This is the dessert. That's because it makes the lives of those who practice it sweeter. Those who are disciplined and practice it regularly know what I mean before they ever read this. They embrace discipline. You can't reach your pinnacle to see your vision manifested without discipline. Discipline allows you the confidence that you have done all you need to do to see your vision and dream made a reality. Discipline constructs your hours, days, weeks, months, and years. With discipline, you stay on track with focused organization by providing the foundation to hold the vision and work steady. It reminds you that there is a price to be paid and the cost of not having it is greater than the cost it took to maintain discipline. Let me give a simple example. Let's say you are a mom or dad that wants your child to be the best they can be. Right now in life that is your passion. Then let's say you stay in bed and sleep late and tell the kiddo to get his own breakfast. How is that investment going to turn out? Not very healthy I assume. By applying discipline, you can rise early and make sure your investment is eating a healthy meal; there by nourishing his mind so your child can be prepared to learn at school.

I use running a lot because that was a passion of mine. If I stayed in every time it rained or snowed, I would have never accomplished my goal of marathon training. I had to discipline my mind and body and use of my time to accomplish my goal.

Look at what The Living Bible says in Proverbs 16:22, *"Plans go wrong with too few counselors, many counselors bring success."* Get counselors and be successful. Look at Proverbs 14:16 (TLB), *"A wise man is cautious and avoids danger, A fool plunges ahead with great confidence."* Center yourself as wise and avoid pitfalls and being too impetuous. Get yourself counselors who will tell you what you need to hear and not just what you may want to hear.

I see all these infomercials. They all tell us what we want to hear and none of them tell us what we need to hear, like how low their actual success rates truly are or how much time you actually must spend working so that in the end it all just evens out. Avoid them. Seek qualified counselors, do your homework, and succeed.

9

CENTERED PEOPLE HAVE DEVELOPED EMOTIONAL INTELLIGENCE

There is much written on emotional intelligence today, but I don't want to get too deep into it. However, to not address it would be a huge mistake. Many centered people were practicing it before it became a popular buzz phrase. First of all, you don't want immature people telling you what to do or leading you into something. I moved from Missouri to New York in 1999, and I found plenty of well-meaning people to tell me how to move and what to expect and how to survive. Then I found it rather curious that none of them had ever made a similar move. How much of that advice do you actually think I listened to? None of it.

> h³ HOWARD'S HELPFUL HINT: *Don't allow someone who hasn't been through the fire to give you advice on how to go through it.*

A mother getting ready to deliver her first baby doesn't need me giving her advice on how to do it. An NFL quarterback doesn't need me giving him advice on how to pass the ball while under a heavy rush. The army doesn't need me telling

Excel at Living a Centered Life 65

them how to run top-secret night operations. Get my drift? If you haven't walked the walk, then don't talk the talk.

For the purposes of this book and what I share with you, I have talked the talk and walked the walk. That's what gives me the credibility in writing this. We would have guest speakers come to our institution and share leadership aspects. My staff would sit with me, and several times different ones leaned over to me and said, "You ought to be teaching this, it's the same stuff you share with us." That is about the time I said okay. I do need to do this. I love coaching people to maturity. I also find emotionally immature people to anger easily—almost baby or child-like. Please understand this point I am trying to make. Choose to respond not react. Responding leaves you in control. Reacting is as a friend of mine says "emotional reflex." Let me say that emotion, when used intelligently, can be a blessing and a tool. Let me also stress that emotion used inappropriately is immature and embarrassing. I have been in meetings where those involved lashed out and raised their voices. I want to point out that even two-year-olds do that. It insults my intelligence to sit in a meeting where people act like that. I find when I work with management teams and coach people with these issues that the following equation is helpful when dealing with potentially emotionally charged issues:

Emotion (Anger) + Issue = Division.

Let me explain. You have an issue at work or with a loved one. The people involved are angry. They feel no one is listening to them. Call the union or attorneys and "start the war," is the battle cry I often hear. They team up with people of like-mindedness and sulk in their anger or sometimes worse as we have seen on the nightly news. These people then lose sight of what the real issue was or is. So what I teach is the following.

You have to take away one portion of the equation to get the right answer. If you take away the wrong portion of the equation, then you have division. If you take away the issue, then people are angry and they don't know why or remember why they are angry. If you take away the anger, then you are left with an issue that you can discuss and find success in. If done improperly, they don't remember what the issue was nor can they develop what's needed to resolve it and they are left with unresolved emotion and anger. Have you ever heard the saying "cooler heads prevailed"? It is because they didn't allow the emotion to influence the outcome. So now the equation should look like this:

$$Issue-Emotion\ (Anger) = Solution$$

Discuss the *issue* remove the *anger* and you get a *solution*. More mature emotions must be chosen for this equation to work. Cooler heads and compromise at times makes for the best and quickest solutions. I have seen angry issues continue for months because emotionally immature people made emotionally immature choices. Getting rid of the anger is a matter of choice. It doesn't matter how we feel. It does matter the choices we make when we don't feel like making the right choices.

I don't allow television to tell me how to think. Just because someone on TV is acting all emotional doesn't make it right. I can think on my own and better without television telling me how to dress, what to drive, what to eat. Develop your emotional intelligence to complete maturity.

Centered People Look for Inspiration

When I need or desire to have centered growth, I always keep my eyes open for inspiration. You find songwriters, poets, inventors, investors, actors, fashion designers, all do the same. To be a centered person with inspiration, I suggest the following four rules:

- Subject yourself to it.

- Look around you.

- Look inside you.

- Share it-Let it out-Watch it grow and mature.

Subject yourself to it. How many of us understand that if we are to be successful investors, we usually have to look for the right things to invest in. Most of the time, the right things aren't necessarily jumping up and down in front of us. When I need inspiration, I do a myriad of things. I go to Barnes and Noble and read magazines and books and I watch people. Sounds a bit odd right? First of all, the magazines and books have more knowledge than I can contain and help me see the flavor of the month or style of the season or at the least keep abreast of the issues that are current. What about music? Music inspires us. Just look at the football games and the music they play over the loud speaker to get the crowd pumped up and into helping their team. Christmas music makes us think about Christ and the holiday season. I bet you won't find too many depressed people listening to Christmas music. Music opens the mind and the soul for inspiration to be received. Music places us in the right frame of mind and spirit to receive inspiration at church and other events. Music transcends the deepest of emotions. Listen and be inspired. Take your laptop to a bookstore and sit in a new environment and type with a different perspective.

Look around you. Remember, I said I watch people. That's right I watch what they wear, how they walk, how they talk, how they smell, eat, drink, etc. People can be very inspirational on what not to do as well as what to do. You don't think so? Then why do we read the newspaper? We read it to of course see the news, but we also read it because we remember loved ones and friends who inspired us and are now in the obituary column. On a happier note we read the sports page to see how our favorite team and players performed. When we see that our team won then we become inspired and happy. Ever see a person depressed because his team won?

Look inside yourself. I look inside myself so often for inspiration and usually find it. This takes time and careful introspection and listening. I'm more comfortable with this place to look because it keeps me in charge. I usually know what I want to do if only I take the time to look within and listen to myself. It keeps me honest as well. To be successful at introspection, one must be grounded and centered. We each know the one thing that does that for us. For me, it's the spiritual side of life. If I have read my Bible and prayed, then look out, world, here I come. If I haven't, it's always on my mind that I need to pay attention to that part of my life. For others it's family. If they see their family is doing well, then they do well and vice versa. Some can't function if all the bills aren't caught up. We all know what it is for us.

Share it-Let it out-Watch it Grow. That's what you invest with the inspiration you have received or discovered. Have you ever noticed when you meet someone that they don't have much to say and they really want to hear what's on your mind? That's the time to invest your thoughts unashamedly by letting it out of the original container, who is you. Then I find the next response so fascinating. I get to watch my inspiration grow as others say, "Oh yeah I had that same thought, and here is what I did." They, in turn, invest in my original thought, and before I know it I have so much inspiration to build upon. I do offer caution here, though. Don't share with those who only take. That's not an investment; it's a charity case—one that you can't see a return on and one that won't give you a return, which is of course worse. I'm not saying they are bad people; they just tend to be people who take and don't give. Therefore you won't see a return and you won't call it an investment.

10

Centered People "CAN" Their Humor

What does humor have to do with being centered? Centered people have things in their proper places, including humor. I would be remiss not to mention it. Don't you love humor? Humor can really lift your day and moment, or it can make you look like a donkey. I have seen people get fired because of their perceived humorous speech. I have seen promotions stop because people couldn't use humor correctly. I have seen people use humor to hide behind their insecurities. We have all seen the wedding toast go badly because someone thought they were being funny. I want to spare you that embarrassment. I saw a car commercial on television where a young man was driving his girlfriend's father somewhere, and the girlfriend was in the back seat. The girl's father was giving the young man the evil eye, which prompted the young man to offer an explanation of "I'm sorry sir, if I had known you were an attorney, I would not have made that lawyer joke." That's funny, but also a good example of how good intentioned humor can go awry. Also, humor doesn't have to be dirty to be funny. In the business and personal world, I don't think there is room for off-colored humor. You should be able to show people your mind is so much better able to think and come up with funny comments that are appropriate. I want to share with you how to use humor.

h³ HOWARD'S HELPFUL HINT: *"CAN Your Humor"*

Can it means humor must be controlled, appropriate, and necessary.

Rule 1: Controlled: Have you heard it said, "Okay, it was funny the first time"? Yes, we all have. That's because the person didn't know how to control it. He or she thinks, "Okay, I got a laugh out of everybody now I need to keep it going," a regular comedian, who falls flat on his face. And the kicker is they usually fall right in front of everyone and look foolish to the whole audience. Actors and good humorists understand that timing and eloquence is the key, not too much and not too little. They know how to read their crowd or room and have developed the necessary self-control to maintain appropriate humor. I have seen people called clowns because no one thought these people could ever be serious about anything. Don't let that be you.

Rule 2: Appropriate: I have met people and been in meetings where people insensitively thought their humor was all that mattered. Let me give people like that a hint: Just because you think it, doesn't mean it's right! These people give off-colored jokes about races, creeds, nationalities, what people are wearing, etc. Oh yeah, they are funny but entirely inappropriate. It would be like someone getting up in front of the Pope and telling Catholic jokes. Let others have their own self-deprecating humor. Not you. I have often said, "If you want to hear the best lawyer jokes, ask a lawyer. If you want to hear the best doctor jokes, ask a doctor." There is a lot of truth in that. If you feel you have to have humor to win a crowd and have favor, make sure it's appropriate.

Rule 3: Necessary: People can have humor at the most inappro-priate times—funerals, weddings, meetings, etc. Have enough sense to know that the event you are attending is special or important to someone. Have even more sense to know when and if it's necessary. Sometimes humor breaks the ice. If you need humor as an icebreaker, then I refer you to Rules number one and two. People aren't going to say "Well, that's just How-ard," or "What a Joker." They are going to roll their eyes and squirm in embarrassment. Then you're going to look foolish.

I don't want to sound all stuck up about humor. I love humor. I love to laugh. I like the comedy channel when they aren't being dirty, but don't take it where it isn't necessary.

11

Centered People Develop
Their Own Mindset

Romans 12: 2 (TLB) states, *"Don't copy the behavior and customs of this world, but be a new and different person with a fresh newness in all the ways you do and think, then you will be able to learn from your own experience how his ways will really satisfy you."*

How a person thinks is so critical to his success. You can be a new and different person with freshness in all you do by transforming your thought patterns. The mindset quickly manifests itself by what people confess and repeat over and over in their minds. I want to invest in you to center and develop your perfect mindset. Have you noticed how an athlete that goes into a game with confidence usually wins? I have seen professional fighters defeated before they entered the ring to fight. I could see it in their eyes. Their mindset was established long before the event began, and it manifested itself during the event. Because of their mindset skills, they often will themselves to a victory over an equally tough opponent. You have also noticed the salesman who has the mindset he or she is there to close the deal. Their approach to the deal came through their mindset and manifested itself in their approach to the customer and in closing the deal. Allow me to make the following suggestions in developing a mindset.

Challenge it. Always challenge your thoughts. Challenge your current ways of thinking. It can be intimidating, but it's worth the price. I ask questions I already have an answer to just so I can hear or see if someone has a better answer than me. I have met a lot of people who are too insecure to expose themselves like that, but I encourage you to be the one that isn't intimidated by it. I think it is a weak, self-centered mind that can't challenge even its own way of thinking. The simplest way is when buying a car. You want a certain car, but you don't believe it's really the right car for you. However, you really want it, and you are ready purchase it until you ask your spouse why you really desire that car when what you really need is a mini-van. That's the second benefit of challenge; it forces us to be truthful with ourselves as well. Scientists and researchers and developers are constantly challenging their findings and their ways of thinking that led them to their discoveries and failures.

Recognize that new ways of thinking are necessary for moving forward. What would the world be like today if man had accepted the fact the model T Ford would be the best car ever built? We certainly wouldn't have landed on the moon with that mindset. What if the mindset standard was that we should all only go to school until the eighth grade? We would all be a bunch of Jethro Bodines. A bunch of Beverly Hillbillies. Understand that to move forward, we need thinkers that challenge our mindsets like Dr. James Dobson who revolutionized the way we look at families. Like Abraham Lincoln and a century later Dr. Martin Luther King who showed us a mindset with racial prejudice and hatred couldn't move a nation forward but only hold it back. Like women who said they should have equal rights, willing to take a stand and change their minds and the minds of others. There are so many others to name. My question now is will your name be listed next as one who changed your mind to move yourself and possibly a nation forward?

Go against your nature. To change a mindset, one has to be willing to be uncomfortable. Let me let you in on a secret. It's okay to be uncomfortable because the growth is worth the small price you are feeling. I will give a simple illustration. How many people like to run? I can see around me everyday people who only run to the kitchen. If one says, "Wait, I'm tired of being overweight. I hate to exercise, but I know it's necessary," that person has just taken a step to become a new and different person in the way they view exercise. Their mindset has now allowed them to move toward success in that area. Exercising wasn't natural to them. However, by adopting a change of thoughts and allowing those thoughts to be expressed through actions, a new mindset begins to develop. With that mindset change, the physical outward appearance will change because the thought produced an action.

Don't be critical. News flash: God didn't give anyone the gift of criticism. The self-anointed critics sit in the cheap seats, never having experienced the price it took a person to do what they do and yet they think they have the "insight" to tell us what we did was wrong. Don't develop a critical mindset. It stops creativity. I look at the national press at times and wonder when they criticize the president, right or wrong, if they have what it takes to walk in the president's shoes. Most don't; I assure you. Don't allow yourself to be so self-righteous that you are critical of others to a fault. Give people a break. Allow them to fail, as well as succeed.

Develop critical thinking skills. Do you see the difference between this and my previous statement? This allows creativity to flow. Learn to look at things critically without having a critical or

demeaning attitude. Doctors and nurses all have critical thinking skills. So do engineers, scientists, CEO's, and VP's. Guess
who else does? Your mom. That's how things progress. They
developed a mindset to view things critically without finding
fault and arrogance and then developed better engines, better
medical cures and better schools and better-prepared children
attending school.

12

Centered People Prepare to Be Chosen

There is a biblical scripture that states many are called but few are chosen. Do you know why they are called? Do you know why few are chosen? Many are called with the inspiration and potential God placed in them. There is a plan they need to be inspired to sacrifice and work out in their life. The natural gifting is there within them as well. Oftentimes, we overlook it because it seems so simple to us we think it couldn't possibly be a gift from God to use to help others. People and businesses are always looking for good, talented people. So now have you guessed why so few are ever chosen? The answer is this. *Few prepare themselves to be chosen.* They also quit before the training is complete. They don't develop themselves with new mindsets, skills, and tools that are necessary to be chosen. Many think that if they shower and shop for new clothes at Macy's and get a nice complimentary hairstyle and look the part, then they should get the part. That's not how it works. Business and organizations today are looking for performers who have prepared themselves and can step in and within a reasonable amount of time be able to be a contributor to the direction the company is heading. I suggest the following steps for preparing yourself to be chosen.

Get the tools necessary. Did you ever try to use a pair of pliers when a wrench was the tool of choice? You may have gotten the job done but wasn't it painful? You may be able to fake your way into the boardroom but without the necessary tools you certainly won't be able to stay there. Have the courage to step out and admit you need more tools and prepare yourself to be chosen. If you need more training or more education or more time, then get it. Go talk to colleges and see if you fit into their educational program to assist developing you.

Develop a reason to be chosen. If I have a job that requires a certain skill set and I have fifty people apply, why should I choose you? What do you offer the company that makes me acknowledge that you are a fit, that you are the one? If I have a project in your company and three people want to be in charge of it, why should I choose you? To be quite honest, when I go to an interview, I don't go answering questions. I go telling them my vision and how it fits with their company and why they want me on their team. They don't have a lot of time to waste interviewing me. You can bring the interviews to a screeching halt in a good way by preparing yourself to be chosen and astonishing them as they hear the vision come out of you as if you already had the position.

Spend your time wisely. If you are developing and desiring more, then don't spend your time on video games and TV. Sure those things and recreation have a place in your life. Make sure your life is ordered in a way that you are spending your time developing and working and not wasting it playing and filled with distractions. Centered people constantly have a passion for what they are doing, and they aren't wasting their time doing things that don't move them towards their passion and goals.

Eliminate Distractions. Centered people know that eliminating distractions isn't a passive step. It's a deliberate aggressive step. Don't allow people or things to interfere with your development. There are a lot of important issues in the world today. None of us can possibly carry the flag for all of them. You choose which ones you want to carry, and don't be distracted by the rest. We aren't here to save the world as much as we are to contribute to it getting saved. You can't be centered and contribute if you allow lesser things to distract you. It's funny that stats say that during the week of the NCAA men's basketball tournament about half of the normal work load is accomplished. That's not good news for those companies paying high salaries to keep moving forward.

Go where the action is. Centered people get in the game. They go where "it" is happening. You can't become more by holding on to the past. Most major corporations aren't in small remote villages. They are in cities that have shipping costs they can afford and a tax base that's supportive of the schools, highways, and civic system. Go there and enjoy the resources and success the action brings. And then become a contributor to it and benefit from it as well.

Do what others won't. Centered people do the hard things and do them right. That's what I call placing yourself in a position to succeed. A lot of people just do what it takes to get by and don't want to make the effort and pay the price for the necessary success. I have often told people of my marathoning days. I ran twelve marathons and multiple other races. When I trained correctly and put in the necessary time and effort to be successful, I ran great races. When I slacked off and did what it took to get by and finish the race, I ran much slower and poor races. In other words, when I chose to do the hard things and do them correctly, I won. When I didn't, I lost. I let myself down by choosing to prepare poorly. It was my choice. Others didn't influence it. The failure was mine and mine alone to own. When I studied properly for exams I did well. When I slacked off, I didn't do as admirably.

Place yourself in a position to succeed. Centered people are constantly placing themselves in a position to succeed. Doing all the above-mentioned steps will do this. But I would be remiss to not tell you that you need to give yourself and others permission to fail as well. People think any failure is the end of the world. I guarantee you it will be okay. Centered people know it won't be the end of the world. You learn much by your failures. I find this a hard message for people to accept. They think they should be positive-minded and not expect failure. The truth is, I have never met a human being who hasn't failed at something in life. If you know of one please send him to me so I can learn from him. Chances are they haven't been challenged on a high enough level to have the opportunity to fail. I have. I have given myself permission to succeed and to fail. The funny thing is that by doing this, I have found I have many more successes than failures and I am less afraid to try new things as a result of fearing I may fail.

Place yourself around successful centered people who you can receive influence from. In closing, I think it important to tell you that it doesn't just take work. It takes *hard* work. Oftentimes, I failed my way to success by ignorance or stumbling upon success. Those times were embarrassing and enlightening to say the least, but they were still successful times only because I was in the game. Place yourself in a position to succeed so that others around you, under you, and over you may succeed as well. Remember others love to share in your success, so let them. Give them your success, and they will become even more than they thought they could. It gets contagious.

13

CENTERED PEOPLE LET THEIR PAST BE THE PAST

Anybody perfect? Never failed? Anyone never experienced personal hurt and pain? Anyone reading this ever come from a home that was poor and lacked finances and clothes and food? Are you one of the people mentioned in the book of Romans who have sinned and fallen short of the glory of God? Anyone ever wish they had done some things in their life differently? Good! Me too. Well then, allow me to welcome you to the family—the human family. Oftentimes we carry regret and allow ourselves to wallow in the mud of self-pity, and this leads to a major break in our level of confidence. One thing I have learned about failure and most hardships is to leave them in the past. I have had failures that can rival most any person's. We have all heard you can't drive a car forward while always looking in the rearview mirror. Well, you can't drive life forward by looking in the rearview mirror of the past. Hindsight is 20/20, however it's done. I never hold someone's past against him because most of the time we can't change it. In doing so, I release myself and that person to go on and be successful in ways he couldn't have imagined. If it were a perfect world, we could all have mentors and teachers who would teach us not to fail and give us nothing but victory. How absurd does that sound? Oftentimes, I find that the reason I fail is because of a stupid decision on my part, not someone else's. Sometimes I'm on teams that fail, and I have ownership in that as well. We all contribute to it in those times. Keep looking forward and most importantly keep moving forward, not being weighted down with thoughts of the past. I watch wrestlers in the Olympics. One wrong move can cost them years of training and a medal because of it. He didn't let this stop him though. He came back and wrestled for and won the bronze medal. He could have beat himself up about it, and we all saw how disappointed he was to have made such an error; however, he left it in the past and lived to wrestle successfully another day. Forgive yourself and leave your failures in the past.

To be successful in doing this you must do what I mentioned in the last chapter about removing distractions. Failures are distractions we take personally and carry in baggage that should just be thrown in the mental trash dumpster. Push the delete button in the computer of your mind and delete the negative thoughts that grind you to a halt. Get rid of them. Stop paying attention to the distracting voices that steal your vision. By faith and hope in yourself and your future, keep placing one foot in front of the other and keep the pace moving forward. Remember earlier in the book when I said the hardest person to know is yourself? Well, my personal experience is that I find I'm also the hardest person for me to forgive. We all need to take times of cleansing and clean out the cycle of failures we incurred. Let them go. Quit holding onto them as if they meet some emotional need and make you feel so bad that you want to cry.

There are always critics to tell you what you should have done or should be doing, what you shouldn't have done or shouldn't be doing. I find some hide in what I like to call "consultants' clothing." I heard a man say one time that a consultant is someone who borrows your watch and tells you what time it is—a lot of truth in that. Then you pay them for it. They are also people you hire and pay to tell others the same thing you have been trying to tell them for years. But they won't hear it from you because, at some point, they know you have failed. Only now, they will listen or accept it from the "professional." Either way, they aren't listening. It is said a prophet is not honored in his own hometown. Why is that? Because the neighbors all know us. They watched us grow up, fail, speed in cars, and do stupid things young people are prone to doing. They saw our youthful exuberance as we sped in cars and spread our wings, and now they don't think we could have possibly grown into a God-fearing, tax-paying, responsible family person and mature professional. They can't believe we could have grown up into something that contributes to society. Don't let that bother you. Don't let the thought of what others say or think be a distraction and hold you in mental chains that keep you from moving forward. Don't allow their feelings to be projected onto you. Don't take it to heart. Let it go, even if they can't. Don't allow their actions towards you to produce a seed of doubt.

> h³ HOWARD'S HELPFUL HINT: *Don't let other people or your past define your future. You determine it and own it.*

14

MEDIOCRITY IS A POVERTY MINDSET

Centered people can't settle for mediocrity; it isn't in them to allow it. When they recognize mediocrity in their lives, it is like seeing dirt on their bodies. They have to deal with it and get rid of it. Centered people can't stand mediocrity. They understand that it is a self-imposed limitation.

> **h³** HOWARD'S HELPFUL HINT: *Centered people live a life of removing self-imposed limitations.*

Being an administrator and having to be accountable for many people who report to me, I have found mediocrity to be a state of norm. I regret the fact that I even have to admit that. I further regret looking back at my own life and seeing areas that I allowed myself to be mediocre in because of my own laziness or ignorance or attitude of just trying to get by. One area I will share with you is the area of education.

In my life, as I mentioned earlier, I dropped out of high school and joined the military. I basically lacked the confidence to be successful at schoolwork because I didn't instill in myself the discipline to do the work. I found most of it to be boring, and I didn't want to be inside when the sun was shining.

I lived in a farm community, and the men weren't inside; they were outside. I had a distorted perception of reality during the high school years like most kids do. At that age, we haven't experienced enough to have a rounded view of life. It wasn't my teachers' or parents' fault. It was mine. Could they have done more and held me more accountable? Maybe perhaps or maybe not. But that's the past. Mediocrity had been my lifestyle. My dreams and desires weren't mediocre. But they would never be manifested as long as I allowed myself to put forth mediocre efforts in all areas of my life. .

Have you seen the so-called reality shows that seem so popular? I was flipping channels and ran across a show called *Nanny 911*. This nanny goes into homes to help dysfunctional families become more functional, or become what I call normal. I was actually in a state of shock watching this family and the father so much in mediocrity in his emotions that the nanny actually told him he was clueless. There are other reality shows that show men needing an intervention because they can't even dress themselves or get a haircut without someone holding their hand and just being normal. These shows try to deliver some people out of mediocrity. I just watch and shake my head and ask questions like, "How in the world do you get that messed up?" I tell you how. They have allowed themselves to stop growing and settled for ways to maintain a lifestyle of mediocrity.

> h³ HOWARD'S HELPFUL HINT: *Centered people take drastic steps to avoid mediocrity.*

Mediocrity may cost you a job interview or, worse yet, something really dear to you. Drunk driving is a sign of mediocrity. Self-centered, not centered people exploit this. At times, being in mediocrity is like being drunk with alcohol; people can't see anything better than the condition they are in.

When I went to college to get an education so I didn't have to make five or six dollars an hour for the rest of my life, I soon discovered I had left out the tools necessary for success. Glaring at me was the fact I still didn't have the discipline to sit still and do the work it took to get better grades. I had the potential and the ability; however, I was wanting success and wanting it now. I applied to several different nursing programs. I felt like my calling in that season of life by God was to be a registered nurse. I noticed in the application form and standards of each school had a paragraph that stated something like "These are the minimum required courses and minimum grades and grade point average one must have to be considered into our program." Most of the time, the minimum standard was a grade of a "C." Since I had a mediocre poverty mindset, I found the only effort I put forth was to just get by. I hope you understand why I am using the word poverty in these sentences. Poverty gives you just enough to get by, and not always will poverty let you get by. If all I needed was a C, I only studied hard enough to get a C. Then, when I sent my transcripts in expecting to get accepted, I found that most people were working hard out of their successful mindsets and getting A's and B's. My grades placed me at the bottom of the stack of those just getting by. I justified it by saying, "Oh you know I work nights. I go to school during the day. It will be okay." Well it wasn't. I was rejected more than twice by several schools. God helped me to wake up and see that I was hurting myself, so I took another year of college improving my grades and grade point average. Finally, one school was accepting its final class. They were going to close the doors after that class graduated. Guess what! I got accepted! Once in the school, I noticed how competitive my fellow students were in striving to be the best. That challenged me, and I had to become better. On top of that, if I didn't, and I struggled, chances were I wouldn't be able to pass the state boards required for licensing and practicing nursing.

Needless to say, I worked harder and harder and made better grades. I had changed my mind from accepting mediocre work to only accepting my best work. I did end up being selected president of that class, and my only claim to fame is that I was the last student to receive a diploma from that historic school of nursing. I then went on to go to another school, Missouri Western State College, and got my BSN in nursing and made the dean's list the semester I took more hours than I had ever taken before. I was working full-time as well. I threw off the self-limitations I had developed as a lifestyle allowing myself to create a new lifestyle. I am so thankful to my instructors and professors there who made me believe that I could do so much better and become so much more than the efforts I had previously put forth. Look at my timeline and see I now have accomplished so much more by getting rid of the mediocrity in my life. You don't do as I did and get your Masters from the University of Missouri Columbia School of Medicine and get appointed by governors to state wide boards and become employed at level I university hospital administration positions and write books by being mediocre.

What I want to impart to you is this: mediocrity is a curse like poverty. Poverty settles for less in every area of life. It is restricting. It could be a deathblow to any dreams and plans. Settling for mediocrity is like watching a sports organization settle for finishing at a .500 level or below year after year. No one wants to be a part of it. They have no conscious intention of searching for ways to reach the highest level. All they want to do is keep a team employed in the market they are in. It's like watching an organization allow its employees to put out infe-rior products or inferior customer service. They tolerate it until finally the customer says forget you and never returns. Then the company goes out of business. Look at the empty seats in the ballparks of the mediocre teams. Look at the negative cash flows of the companies that practice mediocre service quality. It takes no effort at all to be mediocre. It takes no effort to do things half-heartedly.

I urge you personally and professionally to take more pride in yourself than that. Don't wait for others to lead the way in getting out of mediocrity. You take the initiative and say, "No more. No longer will I tolerate performing, speaking, acting, and leading a mediocre life." Others will see the difference, and you may inspire them as well without even knowing you are.

I notice that people who rise up out of mediocrity do so by making conscious decisions to do so. If all else fails, pray and talk to others who are successful and lead a life like you desire. God can and will help you rise out if you so desire. He can and will lead people in your path to bless you and impart to you something that gives you the "aha!" moment and clue you so longingly desired. You will see magazine articles that speak to you and give you insight. The Lord will direct your footsteps towards success and away from that old way of being. That's so inspiring. The change is so worth it.

15

CENTERED PEOPLE CHOOSE TO BE NICE

Wow, what a revelation! I know you think you should skip this chapter. However, just hang with me. First of all, I'm totally shocked I have to teach grown people to be nice to each other, to treat each other the way they want to be treated. Proverbs states that kindness makes a man or woman attractive. Is that you? Attractive? Have you met people who were attractive, but on a closer look they appeared to be plain in their dress attire or how they carried themselves? Perhaps that attraction came from the glow they have by being kind. Their spirit is one of kindness. Many nurses I know have this glow about them. How many of us visited churches where niceness wasn't a trait being manifested? How did that make you feel about ever returning to that church? Perhaps it was a hospital or another organization. I have been shocked to find that when I go to a business and they treat me nice, I stand there thinking, *oh my gosh they are nice!* That is a sad statement on us as a society when being nice isn't the norm but rather the exception.

I find people who say this is a dog eat dog world. For argument's sake let say that's true. I personally don't believe it, but I do see evidences of it. I am around people who see being nice as a weakness. People think if I'm not direct and rude people will take advantage of me. They stand guarded. We have all had that happen. Just try to park at the mall during Christmas rush.

> h³   HOWARD'S HELPFUL HINT: *Choosing to be nice isn't a sign of weakness; it's a healthy choice.*

Quite the contrary, being rude is a sign of weakness and is also a choice, a selfish choice. I have taught my teams and children the next phrase. "I don't care what a customer or acquaintance says or does to you. You have a choice in how you respond." If they are angry, get past the angry part and get to the root of the issue. If both parties are angry, then nothing gets resolved. They have already determined to be nice before the confrontation ever begins.

> h³   HOWARD'S HELPFUL HINT: *Centered people don't let others determine how they respond.*

Don't give others that kind of power in your life. Don't relinquish your power of self-control and responsibility in any area of your life to another person. Athletes have figured this out—all the trash-talking that occurs during a game. Why do athletes trash-talk? One reason is because it works on those who haven't developed good concentration skills. Another reason is because most of the time they are looking at a mirror image of their own talents and are intimidated they might lose in front of everyone. So they try to turn the tables. Some athletes are so arrogant they think they can't be beat, and they just run their mouths. People in society do that as well. I'm actually glad I can't hear half of it. The successful athlete isn't listening to it and taking it personally. They may hear words being spoken, but they have developed such concentration that the trash-talking doesn't penetrate their concentration. You too can develop that. When dealing with customers or family or even business associates, determine to make the conscious choice to be nice or at least appropriate. If it doesn't come easy for you, then "fake it until you make it." Sounds hypocritical but it isn't. Remember you are developing and becoming. So if being too direct is your state of being, then fake being nice until it is a habit of yours of actually liking being nice. You will become that which you practice. Concentrate on the issue not on the anger. In doing so, they see you are listening to their concern and being nice and almost always end up apologizing for their behavior at the end of the confrontation. Of course, you may feel like you were just run over by a Mack truck. That's okay, we all have experienced that. If that's you, take a break and gather your thoughts in a prayer, listen to some music, and refocus. Then take a drink of water and persevere forward with a smile on your face. Sometimes after the Mack truck of life has hit me, people ask me what I am smiling about. I jokingly tell them it isn't a smile; it's a grimace. They get a chuckle out of it because they understand. They have had the same experiences.

16

CENTERED PEOPLE ARE
VISIONARY NOT VISIONLESS

One of the dictionaries defines having a vision as "the manner in which one sees or conceives something." I like that definition. Now let me give you my definition of a vision. A vision is a God-breathed, God-inspired desire that is so real to you before you ever see it fully manifested that you can't help yourself but to see it fulfilled. It is so inspiring to you that you know you won't be the same until you make it happen. I believe God has been inspiring men and women since the beginning of time. I think the issue is it has also become obvious who made a conscious decision to listen and then to work to see that vision accomplished.

The Bible says God is no respecter of persons; so that means anyone can have a vision. Look at Jeremiah 33:3 (TLB), *"Call to Me {God} and I will answer you, and show you great and mighty things, which you do not know."* God himself guarantees that if you seek him and ask, you can take him at his word to show you things you can't yet see. Perhaps it is something about your profession that you seek or new insights into research and development. God wants to show you the secrets he has held special for those willing to pay the price to seek him for them.

Let's discuss how to recognize a vision and work to see it to fruition.

How many people do we see walk around content blending into the public fabric with no concern about a vision or becoming all they can be and to help others become all they can be? I believe they have been given a vision, a purpose, and a dream, but for one reason or another they decided not to pursue it. I want you to do all that is in your power and then some to see your vision, and then see it come alive.

Most people get inspiring, inventive thoughts and think it was just a crazy youthful desire. They write it off as just one of those things or a passing fantasy. They thought, well that's for them, someone else. Someone like me couldn't possibly do that. Sadly then, the inspiration they received is allowed to die by their conscious decision just as quickly as it was born. That seed of inspiration fell upon soil that couldn't birth it and help it grow.

The reason I'm writing this is to make sure you stay centered and that you don't allow your dream and vision to die. I wonder how many songs have gone unwritten and books unwritten and inventions not created, diseases not cured because the dream was allowed to die. I spend my life investing in others and imparting to others. I believe others are my best investment I could possibly make in this lifetime given me. I ask God for better ways of doing that. Since God thinks the same, I don't want to be found doing less. That's my vision by *investing* in others to help them to center themselves and to become all they can be.

17

CENTERED PEOPLE KNOW IT'S
ABOUT WHAT YOU SEE

Mark 9:35 (TLB) states *"Anyone wanting to be the greatest must be the least—the servant of all."* Do you see the wisdom in that statement, or is it another boring scripture to you? Again, it's about what you see. It goes back to your vision. What I see when I read that is if I become a servant–an investor of all—I will become the greatest. Why? What's so special about me? Because I'm a big shot with a big ego? No- it's because if I choose to invest and serve in them, then I become indispensable to them. I have made it so they don't want to succeed without me. They make a place for me because they need me because of my role, which is part of who I am: a servant who always has a place in someone's life. The word servant has taken on such a negative tone by those lacking wisdom and understanding. If God himself says the greatest position is a servant's or service position, then why do we give it such a low place of status and pay it less monetarily. I believe it's because we all want to feel important or be in charge and be the head and not the tail. But I'm telling you to become a servant; invest in and serve others and you will be the head.

h³ HOWARD'S HELPFUL HINT: *Move from being servant to being investor.*

Okay, lets give the title "servant" a new name, "investor." An investor imparts value. An investor finds valuable resources in whatever they are investing. Investors are wise, or they fail. Investors invest finances in the stock market and watch them grow, and they get more money (hopefully). If you invest in people, you get relationships that are so valuable they can't be replaced with just any other relationship. It is so valuable that a price can't be placed upon it. That is the place and reward for an investor.

I also want to add that you aren't made an investor; you become an investor. You make a conscious decision to be an investor. Just like the stock market, you can be an investor that's aggressive or moderately aggressive or a safe investor with minimal risk. You have to have the heart of an investor. You just can't pretend to be something you aren't. You will make yourself look foolish. For instance, I can try to convince myself I'm something I'm not. But the truth is, if I haven't prepared myself by doing the necessary work and preparation and have the right attitude, no matter how much I try to convince myself otherwise, I'm just pretending. The sad part is that others see me lying to myself but don't convince me I'm lying to myself, and they, too, allow me to fail. But it's still my responsibility, not theirs, to be honest with myself.

Who am I? What am I meant to be? Why am I here? What could I possibly contribute? All these questions lead you to your vision of who you are and what you will manifest in your life. I suggest you write these questions down and answer them as honestly as possible. I believe everyone has a vision. I don't think it's always as recognizable as we need it to be. Remember, this is part of learning to know yourself.

Thank God for visionaries like Martin Luther King, Thomas Edison, workers and engineers at the Ford plant. Today, because they paid the price to see their vision produced, I get to enjoy the fruits of their labor. I have electric lights, a running car, and I live in a free society, removing myself from self-imposed racial boundaries. I benefit because they worked to make their visions come to pass.

Again I ask, what is vision? The latest buzz phrase or is it something that can take root and birth forth dreams? I believe that vision is a life force that is necessary to creating and living a life without self-limiting boundaries. Vision is who you are when you want to quit and it seems everything including your family dog is against you. Instead of quitting, a true visionary takes a three-day weekend and recharges the batteries. Your vision is manifested in your job, your speech, and what you do in life and move towards.

Leaders carry a vision that only they can carry, and no one else can do it for them. Why is that? Because the vision was birthed in them and from them. This may sound a tad absurd, but let me illustrate. You can't carry a pregnant woman's baby for her. She has to birth it before you can feel it, touch it, or see it. You all know she is pregnant. You all know she is carrying something. You see her belly sticking out; you see it give a kick occasionally. You are very observant and correct. She is carrying her vision. Believe me, in talking with many women, I have found that she has already seen her baby and envisioned the baby in her heart and mind before her child was born fully manifested to the world. Once born, the baby is her manifested vision, hope, and dream. One that she envisions already playing with, taking to the zoo, reading to, scoring touchdowns, going to college, bringing home a husband or wife and grandchildren. Once birthed, that vision of a child begins to grow and be molded into shape. Like wisdom, knowledge is imparted and care is delivered to ensure safekeeping of her child. Once mature, the process of carrying on the vision and creating a new one continues. Oh yes, people may contribute to that vision in helping it grow and they may attach to it and follow it and relate to it and adopt it as theirs. But it was never their vision. It was the vision of the mothers and fathers who produced it.

Deione Sanders played in a world series and two super bowls. Who had ever performed that before him? I'll tell you who, no one. Deion had the vision to be a professional two-sport athlete and excelled at being who he was at the highest level of the sports he participated in—his vision. When he told others his plans, there were many who said no way. His ego is bigger than his talent they said. It's hard enough to be good at one sport with the dedication required, let alone two that have overlapping seasons where he played both in the same week. But you see, that was Deion's vision, and he let no one else determine it for him. The critics dared to limit him. He didn't accept their constricting limits.

You can find men and women all throughout history who carried and birthed a vision. Do you ever wonder, as I do, how many had a vision they never physically saw manifest? Did others catch it? Were they able to pass it on to another to make it a reality? My heart also grieves at times when I look at prisons, and I wonder how many visions will never be manifested because of human injustice to another person. When I read the newspaper and I see young people die prematurely because of drugs and alcohol, I wonder what song just went unsung and what book just went unwritten. What vision just perished? Were they to be the one to make the next coolest invention? Now we will never know the contribution that was supposed to have been made. We may never know, but allow me ask you: what is your vision? Is it a dream? A fantasy? Or is it the real deal? You know the answer. Choose to be honest with yourself.

I have a test to put it to so that you can know. A fantasy is an action that can never come to pass because it stays in your imagination. It can never be manifested because there is no way possible you could ever do it. A dream and a vision have the substance of hope and faith in it so it can become manifested. You can actually see a vision happening; whether you have the courage to make it happen or not is another matter.

A fantasy of mine was to be a pro football player. When I was in sixth grade, I could see it in my mind throwing and running for touchdowns. However physically gifted I am; I'm not big enough to be a pro football player. I can score all kinds of touchdowns in my mind, but I can never manifest it in reality because I don't have all the physical tools. You see, a fantasy has missing components. A vision isn't missing the components even when you don't have all the answers. Think about that. Meditate on that. Place action to it.

18

CENTERED PEOPLE STRIVE TO SEE THEIR VISION MANIFESTED

To make your vision a reality, you need to plant it, water it, and keep the weeds out. Weeds are the things that choke the life right out of things planted. Avoid them by planting your seed of vision in good soil, and when the weeds come up remove them at all cost. A close friend can poison your vision. He or she can discourage you from pursuing your dream. Then it just lays dormant or dies. Even though people often mean well, there are times they can't believe in your vision because they can't see themselves performing it so they think you can't possibly do it. They think higher of themselves than they do of you. Only share it with people you can absolutely trust and only after it is born, so when you speak of it, it already sounds like a reality. I have shared things with people who treated me that way. I have also shared them with people who said. "Hmm okay," and they took a wait and see approach with me and did not offer any words to discourage me no matter how far-fetched it sounded. My brother-in-law, Ed Simpson, is that way, a godly, trustworthy, honorable man. Ed has been such a blessing to me by responding as he has. His wisdom was to wait and see if Howard actually pulls this off. His wisdom was also not to discourage me from moving that direction unless he knew from the Lord it wasn't for me.

So many times people don't make their vision come true because they are waiting for the television or others to tell them what to think or how to think. They fear success and they fear failure or risks. If we watch it passively, we become the person someone else wants us to be by thinking the way they want us to think. Someone else is programming programs to make us think the way they want us to think. We only see what they want us to see or hear what they want us to hear. We tend to then settle for that which they tell us or show us.

> h³ HOWARD'S HELPFUL HINT: *Learn to settle for nothing less than God's best for you.*

We need to learn to see and think for ourselves with minimal influences that are just selling us. We each are our own person with our own lives to live, with our dreams to dream, and lives to build. Radio plays what they want us to hear; TV plays what they want us to watch. I am choosing to not be that passive but to be deliberate in what I let my eyes see and my ears hear. Centered people control outside influences into their lives. You do this at times without even thinking about it. You go to the mall to one certain store to buy that certain item. You walk past 100 stores not even paying attention to their displays because you have your mind set on that one thing in that particular store. You didn't allow anything else along the way to influence you or change your direction.

Of all the shows we watch on television, how many do you think are actually presented because the programmer cares for us? Once we see that the programmers and sales people are actually showing us what their dream or vision is (i.e. higher profits), we can begin to set ourselves free to develop a new mindset. The power is within us to develop mindsets that are free to explore and be creative and, at the same time, allow us to control the decisions we make. The emotions solicited from watching TV are unfulfilling and are made to influence how you should feel. Since when did we decide to be that passive and let others tell us how to feel? I'm smart and intelligent; I don't need them telling me how to feel or what to believe. I can do that on my own. Your emotions being based upon your thoughts, desires, and dreams are real, nothing less. They are real because they belong to you and no one else. You are free to express them however you choose because they are yours, developed from within you, unsolicited from anyone but God, with no input but his and those you trust.

19

CENTERED PEOPLE KNOW IT'S ABOUT WHAT YOU HEAR

Have you ever spoken something to someone and left thinking they understood what you said. Perhaps your children or coworkers or spouse. Then, to your surprise, you find out from their response that they did not at all understand nor hear what you said. In reverse, I have left meetings and relationships thinking I understood what the person told me, then came to find out that I totally missed it. It can be embarrassing to say the least. Studies have shown us that little children, when being scolded by an adult, cannot hear what the parent is trying to tell them because all they see and hear is a rather large person angrily yelling. They then naturally shut off their listening capabilities out of fear.

I have learned it is just as important to learn to hear as it is to learn to see. Listening has long been a skill we have been urged by scholars to master. To demonstrate this, when I'm speaking to groups of people, I use a technique with music. I play a song or portions of a song on a CD to the group. Then I ask for brave audience members to tell me what they heard. I can tell you most of the time all of the people heard the same song but not the same thing. I then train them to listen for certain things in the song. Most of the time, we hear the wonderful accompaniment of a song—every instrument all-inclusive, all together rocking out. I then have the audience pick out and only listen to the bass or treble parts or percussion parts. To their amazement, they never noticed how individualized the pieces being played really were. They also never realized how the different pieces brought together make a wonderful finished product.

I find pastors of churches that are active and vibrant and full of life are doing this same thing. They are investing in their members, encouraging them to express themselves as God intended them to. They are trying to bring all the parts of God's body together, no matter how individualized the people are and have them performing as the body in harmony. The pastor has each member playing his tune as God has gifted him and helping to move the church body forward.

It validates the following points that centered people do:

> **h³** HOWARD'S HELPFUL HINT: *Centered people hear what they listen for.*

Oh you may have also thought you heard other things, which I assure you that you did. However, you only selectively heard what you intended to hear or looked to hear.

> **h³** HOWARD'S HELPFUL HINT: *Centered people know that listening and hearing are not passive but active engagements.*

Listening requires active participation. If you passively listen, you may miss the intent. You can't hear without being attentive and developing the skill of listening. This requires one to get outside of his own thoughts and intentionally learn to not filter what he has heard through his personal filters such as life or experience or other reference points.

> h³ HOWARD'S HELPFUL HINT: *Centered people develop into LEADERS.*

Having a vision and being a leader are two aspects that go hand in hand. Centered people can't help but become leaders because all the ingredients are there for the leadership role to fall on them. They don't always however, accept that role. I do also want to point out that one can't have a vision and see it become a reality without being a leader who fights and works through the odds to see the vision become a reality.

The words visionary and leader are two words that I believe are overused. They are not the same words. They should however, be used hand in hand with each other. My experience is that too often we find people who are self-proclaimed visionaries and self-proclaimed leaders. I suggest that people should develop or grab a vision and become a leader by leading the process that's necessary to be successful. Then we should let others bestow on us the title of "visionary" or "leader" if one feels the need to have such a title. I have noticed that true visionaries and leaders don't need to be told who they are or what they are because they are too busy working towards seeing their goals happen to care what others think of them, good or bad. Most of the time, they don't even care if people notice them. It's the vision and attaining the end result that is important to them, not the title or fame. Those things will come once what you have accomplished and set value to your vision. You won't have to pursue fame or fortune. It will come to you in many forms once you birth your vision. Others will catch a glimpse and jump on the bandwagon and assist you in your success. Centered people understand this concept and welcome it..

20

CENTERED PEOPLE HAVE A PASSION

Passion is the driver of centered people. Their passion is evident in their approach to their goals and dreams. Not to sound coy, but they are passionate about their passion. I have spoken to many successful people. People who are successful writers, publishers, managers, athletes, principals, teachers, doctors, lawyers, and mechanics all have told me they were just living out their passion and dream. Race car drivers are passionate about their sport of racing. I spoke to author Joseph H. Badal, the author of the books *Terror Cell* and *The Pythagorean Solution*. Joseph recently sold the movie rights to one of his books. He served in the New Mexico State House of Representatives and served in the military in top-secret positions. Joseph has had a passion for writing novels. When he was attending a book signing for his new release at the Harvard University Bookstore in November of 2004, we discussed what it took to be successful at writing. He told me the one key ingredient in authors he saw get published was their passion to write and passion to persevere to get published.

> **h³** HOWARD'S HELPFUL HINT: *Develop the passion to persevere.*

He said those without passion always allowed excuses to stop them from even starting writing. People would tell him how much they too desired to write a book or novel; however, they could never find the time. He and I agreed that our passions make us find the time. We have to go write and work towards our passion with unending perseverance. At times when I was writing this book, I would write into late night or early morning because I loved the flow that was coming out of me onto the pages as I wrote. It was intoxicating and spiritual at times. It was also hard work and draining. Times that the inspiration was not flowing, I persevered. Nothing was going to deter me as this was and is my passion.

To further illustrate this, I will tell you of when I used to train for marathons and run races. It didn't matter how early, or what the weather was like for my training partners, Kevin Bocquin and Rick Hartigan, and me. We allowed for nothing to interfere with our training to have successful races. We were running at 4:00 in the morning to beat the summer humidity Missouri was famous for. We ran in snow, rain, and wind because we needed to train, and we couldn't allow anything to compromise our preparation. We were investing time, sweat, pain, and effort into something only we could envision. I loved to run. I wasn't the fastest or the slowest, but it was my passion. I envisioned myself crossing the line at the New York City marathon and raising my hands as I finished and received my finisher's medal. On Saturday morning, we would be running races and be nearly half-way through before most people were out of bed. Nothing would we allow to deter us from training to reach our goal. We even ran when sick and when the heat index was 105 or higher. I don't recommend that, but we knew what we could handle physically. It was our passion. We were centered. Our passion centered us. Our passion focused us. I had close friends laugh at me jokingly and say they were running to the kitchen. I knew they were kidding around. I also saw the look of admiration in their eyes as they had a friend who completed some of the toughest races known.

> HOWARD'S HELPFUL HINT: *Be a well-centered person that when one passion comes to an end, you can develop and fulfill a new passion.*

What do I mean by this? My actual life passion is to serve the Lord in everything I do. I really don't care what activity it is I do. I have chosen those I believe are for me to do. They just aren't happenstance. My joy is in serving God not in the actual task necessary to be successful. I don't want to fail him and forfeit the life that may have been mine. So as I mentioned running was a passion. It takes a lot of mental physical emotional energy to perform at a high level day in and day out. Add years of running on top of it and you can see how we don't see the same names every year winning races. I never thought I would quit running marathons. However, I have. I learned I was an endurance athlete more than I was a runner. I learned that my passion for running hadn't been lost. However, I was mentally and emotionally tired and needed a new focus to place my efforts towards.

I find centered people who have centered themselves in the proper centered value aren't shaken from who they are when the time comes to find a new passion. They just move on because they are centered in the right priorities. You see, serving God in all areas of my life is my center; out of that flows new and exciting passions God places in my heart and mind to develop and attain. He has a pleasure in seeing us perform at high levels. It gives him pleasure to see his creations excelling while he is an active participant in their lives. I see this in Olympic and professional athletes who had a tremendous passion for the sports they played. When age caught up to them they finished their college degrees, law degrees, doctorates. They are contributing to society with a new passion that they are manifesting in their state of being centered.

Centered People have lives not just jobs.
When hiring new employees, I have always looked and listened for their passion. I could instantly tell who just wanted a job and who actually had a passion for the career. Can you see the difference? I found people who had a strong passion for the career stayed later, came in earlier, were friendlier, and were approachable. Have you ever had someone tell you to get a life? Well, these centered people have a life, not just a job. They knew who they were and what they were called to do during that season of their life. People without passion came with an attitude that they deserved the job because of seniority, good looks, or the fact they met minimum qualifications. Remember, I said I write this from experience. I have been guilty of looking for the job and not being passionate about it. I find that people who live like this aren't centered because they don't know who they are or where they are going. I don't, however, find fault with people searching out the job to see if that sparks the passion in them they are looking for. I admire the fact they are risking it in their search for life. Oftentimes people searching find their passion and become very successful at it and contribute to their communities and us all. What are you passionate about? What makes you smile when think about it? What can you not pass up in life? What do you have to do in order to make it happen?

> **h³** HOWARD'S HELPFUL HINT: *Passionately pursue your passion.*

Don't let another day go by without some movement towards your deepest heart's desires. God placed them there because he knew you were capable of accomplishing them. Now be the steward of the dream and passion and make it manifest so others may be equally blessed. If your passion is to become a teacher, then pursue it. There will be children only you can reach in the way only you can reach them. If it is to be in the ministry, pursue God with all your heart, soul, and mind. Perhaps it is to finish your college degree, to get a better paying job, to raise your family on, and provide for the children's college and future. Then find out what it takes and make the necessary sacrifices to attain it. Bring it from a desire to a reality. *Pay the Price.* It will only be for a season. Then it may allow you to move on to attain higher goals you find you are passionate about.

I hope this chapter has made sense to you. I hope it challenges you to think and reach for your goals and passions. I truly desire for all the readers of this book to attain everything they dream in reality.

Can you imagine a society where all the people attained their passion and contributed to society in such a way that their community and all the people they come in contact with are blessed? Is it pie in the sky thinking? Perhaps, but if it is pie in the sky thinking it is because people aren't willing to pay the price. I challenge us all to that goal.

21

CENTERED PEOPLE ARE HOLISTIC PEOPLE

Understanding that people are holistic is not a new concept with me. Holistic means that you can't treat one aspect of a person's life without affecting all the other parts of their life. I am a registered nurse. I worked as an ER and trauma nurse for years. During my training, I was taught to treat others holistically. The definition is almost self-explanatory, but the medical professions refer to holistic as treating the mind and body—not separating them into parts, realizing that the affects of one can affect the other. I like what the Webster's dictionary says about it. It says it's "emphasizing the importance of the whole and the interdependence of its parts, concerned with wholes rather than analysis or separation into parts."

When we take care of a patient, we are also taking care of their family. Their family hurts as well, and they are concerned about their sick or injured family member. This is especially serious when taking care of newborns and new moms and dads and the elderly who have been married for fifty years. To have their family member sick or injured is like losing a right arm. They are losing a part of who they are and who they have become. They are in all sense and purposes, "like one." When you encourage someone who seems discouraged, you are treating their spirit and their body. Their bodies will react to the condition their spirits are in.

We are very complex individuals making up one whole part. God developed and created us as multifaceted human beings in his likeness and image. For your success, I want to concentrate on helping you to develop a new mindset and approach to your life. I want you to see yourself holistically. I want to assist you and give you the tools to manage your life holistically.

Holistic Categories

Allow me to share with you my categories. These categories reflect who I see myself as being and becoming until I reach my state of self-actualization in each of these areas. What is self-actualization? Mazlow describes it as "the highest attainment a person can realize when they are able to fulfill their potential unhindered by society or circumstances."

My categories are:

- Spiritual
- Physical
- Mental/Emotional Mindsets
- Family
- Financial
- Professional
- Rest and Recreational

You may find you have more categories or want to condense this list to tailor it to your needs. Again feel free; this is about becoming who you are and recognizing you didn't end up somewhere by happenstance or mistake. It gives you the freedom to design your life; watch it unfold before you as you take the steps to design it in faith. You are making a conscious decision of paying painstaking detail to who you are and desire to become.

You have established a design to build a holistic life. You aren't leaving out any categories that are important to you. Others close to you will benefit from your design as well because you have brought order to your life. You won't be a taker but rather are positioning yourself to be a giver, a contributor, an investor. You may say to yourself, "Wait a minute; I have already blown it or missed it by messing up an area of my life." Let me encourage you that it's okay. We all have blown it at some point. The successful people just didn't stay in the puddle of mess made when they blew it. They made a decision to get some emotional healing and move on and grow.

> **h³** HOWARD'S HELPFUL HINT: *Journal your journey.*

I suggest you begin by establishing and keeping a journal. Now, this isn't a conventional journal where you write your thoughts for the day, week, or idea you have. Rather, the mindset of a journal I want you to develop is that of a journal that guides and tracks your vision and life. This journal will be used to keep you focused and on track so that you will gain the ability to generate and birth new ideas. It is also great for measuring where you were to where you are now. Here is an example. Thinking holistically, let's start with who you are and what you desire spiritually and move through the other categories as well. Begin by taking an inventory of where you currently are in all these areas. Don't be intimidated to face the facts. The inventory should encourage you as you realize this is the start; It's not where you are finishing.

> HOWARD'S HELPFUL HINT: *Centered people don't forfeit the good life that could have been theirs by failure in any of these areas.*

h³

What do I mean by this? Having a lackadaisical approach to any of these areas could cost one dearly and possibly irreparably. I don't want this to scare us. I want it to help us take a sober, thought-provoking look at each area, not leaving any detail unattended. The time is now, not tomorrow. Have you seen football announcers talk about Peyton Manning and his success? They show the behind the scenes work he puts into studying his opponents, looking for weaknesses to exploit. He also studies film of himself, paying special attention to what he could have done better so he won't make the same mistake twice. All this is done in private before Peyton steps out into the spotlight of Monday Night Football in front of the whole nation. He isn't going to forfeit his dream and his victories because of his lack of approach. Read Proverbs 24:3–4 in the Living Bible. *"Any enterprise is built by wise planning, becomes strong through common sense, and profits wonderfully by keeping abreast of the facts."* In other words, you can be successful by wise planning, seeking others input, strong by using common sense, such as stay out of bad debt and out of bad markets, reap profits by knowing the facts, the ins and outs of your particular business or field. *Centered people know it is all in their approach.*

Spiritual

I don't care who we are, we are all faced with the question of a higher being and higher calling than merely serving an existence that just ends because we were told that we evolved from monkeys or tadpoles. Your spiritual life is important because this is who you truly are. The spiritual aspect of your life defines your being, the reason why you believe you exist, and what you were put on the earth to do. It establishes why you believe you were created. It places you in touch with yourself and your God, the creator of the universe. It allows you to establish your course with confidence and gives you the assurance you are moving in the right direction as your steps are unfolding in front of you. I have people tell me, "I don't know if I really believe in all that spiritual stuff." What they are really telling me is "Don't bother me with that spiritual stuff; I want to live like I want to live." In II Peter 1:15–16 (TLB), Peter states,

> I intend to keep sending these reminders to you, hoping to impress them clearly upon you that you will remember them long after I'm gone. For we have not been telling you fairy tales when we explained to you the power of our Lord Jesus Christ and his coming again.

We aren't living in a fairytale. God actually parted the Red Sea. He also actually sent his son to be born a virgin birth. He also saw to it that the walls of Jericho fell, and he actually lead his people in to the Promised Land. It's not a fairytale. It is life to all who find it. For me, the scripture Jeremiah 29:11 in TLB is one of my foundational scriptures. It reads, *"For I know the plans I have for you says the Lord. Plans for good not for evil. To give you a future and a hope. And in that day when you seek me and seek me with all your heart, I will be found by you says the Lord."* That scripture tells me that I was created for a purpose. That God himself, the very creator of the universe, has plans for me. It is the same God Moses, Aaron, Jesus, Paul, and David all prayed to. Amazing isn't it?

That same God you read about is listening to us and has a design for us as well. Not only does he have plans but good plans, for a future and a hope. I know some of you find this hard to believe because you believe those were special people. Let me ask you this. Since God is your Heavenly Father, do you really believe he likes one of his children better than another? He isn't like our natural parents who have a finite way of loving. His ways of loving are infinite, and he never changes. The scripture says he is no respecter of persons. He doesn't like David or Moses better than you. He loves us all. Now is the time to settle that issue. Know in your heart that he loves you and desires good for you.

Now that we know he loves us, it still doesn't alleviate our responsibility to the process. It's not passive. I have to perform an active role. You see what it said. It says, "When I seek him." I can't leave him out; I can't leave out the spiritual portion of my life, think I'm whole, and succeed to the ultimate calling. I don't like hearing any pastors refer to us as "lay ministers." I understand they are referring to people who aren't full-time in the ministry. However, I can't separate my spiritual life from any other aspect of my life, and my life is a ministry. Neither can you. My secular profession may not be full-time in the "ministry," but that doesn't mean it isn't my ministry. I don't like being placed in that box, like I am just a second-hand minister or a lesser kind of minister or that I may not count in the total count of ministers. I don't believe God sees it that way. I also believe that discourages people in the body of Christ from serving because they have been made to feel unworthy. We need to watch our language and not issue limiting parameters on people discovering and creating their lives in Christ. After all, Paul was a tentmaker, Luke was a physician, Matthew a tax collector. I don't recall them being labeled as lay ministers. If anything, they were recognized as first disciples then apostles. They were recognized by their gifting.

My part in being centered in Christ is to seek him and that spiritual life he has for me and discover those plans. Read Proverbs 16:1–3. It states in The Living Translation, *"We can make our plans, but the final outcome is in Gods hands."* Verse 3 states, *"Commit your work to the Lord, then it will succeed."* Look at verse 9, *"We should make plans-counting on the Lord to direct us."* Even the writer of Proverbs understood that he had a role and God had a role.

> h³   HOWARD'S HELPFUL HINT: *It is possible to believe that God wants more for me than I want for myself.*

Wouldn't any good father want that for his child? That's why this area is number one and so crucial to our beliefs and our lives' success. First of all, we are spiritual beings. When our bodies give out and die and we pass on to an after life, we don't stop here. We move on in eternity with the sum total of what we invested in our life spiritually. That's why this area is so crucial to your life's successes. The promise God gives to those who seek him is nothing less than the best. Hebrews 11:6 (TLB) states, *"You can never please God without faith, without depending on him. Anyone who wants to come to God must believe that there is a God and that he rewards those who sincerely look for him."* God doesn't know how to give less than the best to his people. That's who he is and what he promises. We were created; we are his vision. To create a people whom he could invest in and who would in turn love him back. He paid the ultimate price by giving us his best, the life of his son.

We were created for a purpose. It's revealed to those of us with the courage and patience and diligence to seek it out and manifest it. God doesn't make mistakes or allow things to happen by happenstance. He has a plan, and so should you. God doesn't treat us like robots. We all have a will to do what we want. God doesn't come against that very often. The reason is because we won't let him. Remember our spiritual value is our uniqueness to us and so precious it should be reserved only to be shared with those we trust with our lives. I'm not saying don't share your faith. I'm saying the most personal aspect of your faith you are growing in is so precious you should only share it with those who have a commitment to you and your well-being. Otherwise, they may not understand and be very critical of you and cause you to stop in that area. You don't want that, so be wise. Now let's take a look at an example of how to create our life's spiritual plan.

Spiritual

- Goal: To have a vibrant, active, relevant relationship with God.
- Steps to attain goal:
- Read my Bible daily.
- Read an inspirational writing daily.
- Listen to music that keeps me in tune spiritually.
- Share my faith with others.
- Pray and have a relationship with God.
- Learn to recognize God's leading in my life.
- Participate in an active, vibrant church as a member.
- Evaluate and Reflect: Measure my accomplishments.
- Did I meet my goals?
- Am I more diligent today than I was yesterday?
- What do I need to do differently?

It's important to remember these are your holistic values. These are yours to design. They come from you and how you see yourself. These are the vision of you. Someone else doesn't create these so that you fit into a certain mold. You aren't being placed in a self-limiting box. These are yours. Be creative. Have fun!

Physical

To be at our best, we have to take care of our bodies. I'm sure you're saying, "Oh boy, tell me something I don't know." Okay, guess what? We all know it but how many of us are taking the time to place ourselves in a position to be successful physically. I'm not saying you have to become a professional athlete. I'm saying you have an obligation to take care of yourself so you can be at your best at all times and that your destiny depends on it. I'm disappointed in myself when I neglect my body and am stuck with the results. Just look at the surveys of the fattest cities in the USA. Look at the surveys of the healthiest cities in the USA. Now I don't believe the city or location has anything to do with it. We tend to be heavier when we don't eat right or exercise no matter where we live. Because our tendency is to be like electricity, we take the path of least resistance. To be at our peak and to be healthy, we have to have resistance. Our immune system resists sickness and disease. Our muscles build when using resistance. Interesting how God designed that to work isn't it? We actually become weak when we aren't challenged in the physical area.

You don't have to go to extremes or run marathons to reach your personal peak. However, like the other areas, we must pay attention to it in order to reach our vision. Develop the vision of what physical condition you want to see yourself in. Don't settle for something you aren't. Take the time to develop a plan and work it through one step at a time to reach your goal physically. Once I put up a picture of a well-built bodybuilder and used it for inspiration.

Physical

- Goal: To be healthy and maintain an active lifestyle
- Purpose: To reach my destiny by physically being able to constantly be at my best
- Steps to attain goal:
- Walk two miles a day three times a week
- Get plenty of rest.
- Eat healthier meals.
- Eat healthier snacks.
- Get a physical from my doctor.
- Take vitamins.
- Lift weights three times a week.
- Control and manage my weight.
- Keep a record of my progress.
- Make it fun!
- Evaluate and reflect: Did I meet my goals?

Were they realistic?
Was it fun?
What do I need to change?

Remember: We all don't have to be Lance Armstrongs. The important thing is to know who you want to be physically and make a plan and work to get there.

Mental/Emotional

This category is critical to your well-being. Have you ever noticed someone who has a great positive mental outlook or status? You notice that their countenance is bright, kind of reflecting or illuminating a light that is born inside of them. Their eyes are wide open. They look forward to the day with the anticipation of a child looking forward to Christmas. They are looking forward to living and conquering new heights. Taking care of yourself mentally and emotionally has several aspects and benefits. The intelligent centered person reads books and studies. The mental aspect I want you to think about is developing a new mindset. Becoming a new person with a fresh newness in all the ways you do and think. Romans 12:1–2 tells you to do this by transforming your thoughts and thought patterns.

That's right; you can become a new person. Are you the same person you were at eighteen? If you are older then let's hope not. We are who we think and believe we are. All thoughts are substance. They have a form in your mind. They are the hope of what you see yourself becoming. You see those aspects in the mind. If I put a baseball uniform on but don't believe I'm a baseball player what has changed? Nothing. But wait, I'm dressed like a baseball player doesn't that make me one? No, I never was a baseball player. People will walk by me and see me and think to themselves "there's a baseball player," but in my mind I'm not a baseball player and I know it. But outwardly I'm sending everyone else a different message. If I really want to be that baseball player, then I need to not only wear the uniform but also set my mind, will, and emotions to pay the price of becoming that baseball player. To become what I want to become, I must control my mental and emotional thoughts. As mentioned earlier, my mindset has to change. I have to become a new and different person by thinking differently and establishing a changed mind.

> **h³** HOWARD'S HELPFUL HINT: *When I think differently, I believe differently, I behave differently, I become different, and I see different, exciting new outcomes.*

I have now established a different way of being because I established a different way of thinking. This allows you the freedom to grow more than you ever thought possible.

Remove the Old Mindsets

> **h³** HOWARD'S HELPFUL HINT: *Centered people know they have to remove the old mindsets to be successful.*

This will be hard because we tend to have walked in old ways of thinking so long that they have become our reality. We tend to believe people who said negative things about us, and we allowed those negative statements and thoughts to stick to us like glue and restrict us from moving forward in our dreams and visions. You also can't just remove one without replacing it with a new mindset.

Developing a new mindset is essential and takes time. It is not an overnight change. It takes time and must be calculated and purposeful by design. More importantly, it's personal, extremely personal. Don't share it; become it. Why not share? Because this is your way of thinking. It's your own personal thoughts. Don't let others mold and shape your thoughts until they are firmly established. You don't want just anyone to lead you down a path that could end up in the death of your dreams just so they could see theirs fulfilled. Now it is okay to solicit thoughts and ideas from others, but place them into your context. What do they mean to you? How does their way of thinking fit and apply to your situation? I ask questions I already have answers to just to see if there is a better way to ask the question or get ideas that may be fresh and different than my own. This isn't insecurity. I'm quite secure in my beliefs and thoughts. However, I am always leaving myself open to new ways of thinking and refreshing my thoughts.

Romans 12:2 (TLB) *"Become a new and different person with a fresh newness in all the ways you do and think."*

Goal: To develop clear thinking patterns to make wise decisions.

Steps to Attain Goal:

- Stay away from toxic people who sabotage.

- Develop algorithmic thinking. Steps 1, 2, 3.

- Gain insight into successful people's ways of thinking.

- Renew my mind daily by reading a spiritual book.

- Actively fight negative thoughts.

- Look for ways to think differently.

- Subject myself to creative thinkers.

- Listen to stimulating music.

- Evaluate and Reflect: Measure changes.

- Are my mindset goals reasonable?

- Is my thinking clearer today than yesterday?

- What do I need to do differently?

- Am I open to new ways of thinking?

It's important to realize that not all mindsets go away instantly. It's been a pattern of thinking over time, and little by little those old negative mindsets can be overcome by replacing them with new positive ways of thinking.

Family

You will make no greater investment in your lifetime than investing in your family. Your family is a direct reflection of who you are and what you have established. The level of commitment you have made in your family will be evident to all, whether we see it or not. The most prized possession, responsibility, and privilege you will ever have is your family. Not only will you be a blessing and investor to them while having a place in their lives, but they will return a blessing to you as well. You reap what you sow. Sow love and reap love. Sow time and reap time. The key to remember is that there are seasons in your family—seasons of infancy, toddler years, grade school, middle school, high school, college, career, and marriage. You only have so many seasons to invest and have a level of influence in their life. Make it count. The kids that once ran to you when they came home, now may barely speak to you as adolescents. They struggle with all the new voices telling them what they should wear, what music they should listen to etc. I suggest you stand firm but loving. I have raised two wonderful children, and I speak from experience. It's a fine line to walk to allow teenagers the space they need to learn who they are and still receive influence from you in a way that stays with them. There are no guarantees but no matter what you believe everyone has a free will and makes their own choices. They all have ownership and responsibility in it as well. They have a will to choose and become who they want to be. Just stand firm and love.

What we are talking about here is investing and staying with your investments until they mature and offer a return. You stay with it for the long haul no matter if it's peaking and giving a return or whether you believe it's on a downslide and costing you. You will experience all those seasons. The New Living Translation Bible tells us in I Corinthians 10:13:

> But remember that the temptations that come into your life are no different from what others experience. And God is faithful. He will keep the temptation from becoming so strong that you can't stand up against it. When you are tempted, he will show you away out so that you will not give in to it.

In other words, you aren't the only one to have ever gone through it or the only person currently going through it. Whether it's sin or just the challenges of life, others have gone through it as well. I find if I open up to other parents about my children and the struggles we face that they in turn are inclined to open up to me as well. Once they learn they can trust me, they open up, trusting I won't hurt them or judge them. Your family is the best investment you will ever make. Have you seen the grief families go through when they have a teenager who suffers a premature death or goes to jail because of a bad choice? The pain and the grief those families experience is beyond belief.

I have witnessed this firsthand as an emergency department nurse. The parents wonder why and what if. They feel like failures. They feel like all life has suddenly come to a screeching halt. I am being serious and writing this so that you may understand the seriousness of this investment, whether its discipline, financial, personal, talk, transportation, sports. Guard it, watch over it, and protect it. Love it. It will save you heartache and has the potential to blossom into a strong love bond that's unbroken, all because of the untiring investment you made into it. And may I also add how much I admire parents who have sacrificed in love for their children. I saw a whole generation of parents who couldn't wait to get their kids out of the house once they turned eighteen and graduated high school. That generation of kids compensated by making sure they didn't do that to their kids and gave their kids more than they were given. Those generations of children have learned to be thankful and face adversity with love in their hearts. I assure you, God knows our failures. He knows, he forgives, he encourages, he walks with us, not against us.

> h³   HOWARD'S HELPFUL HINT: *Relax, God didn't call us to be perfect, He called us to be His.*

Family

- Goal: To have a healthy family

- Steps to attain Goal:

- Spend time with all family members letting them know how important they are and that they are loved.

- Listen to their needs.

- Pray for and with my family daily.

- Invest my free time with my family.

- Listen to my spouse and get his perspective on how well the family is doing.

- Make sure the spiritual and physical and emotional needs of my family are being met.

- Children are grown. Do they need me differently now? Ask them.

- Evaluate and reflect: Am I being successful?

- Is my family spiritually, physically, and emotionally healthy?

- Am I a better spouse today than yesterday?

- Am I a better parent than yesterday?
- What do I need to do differently?

It's important to remember that families are the best invest-ment anyone will ever make. We see our successes and failures in our families. That doesn't mean that you are responsible for them, nor should you feel guilty about them. Love covers over a lot of wrongs. That love is what all families remember.

Financial

The area of finances is so important. As we all know, it takes money to attain the lifestyle we desire. We also know that the lifestyle we desire may not be the one we actually can attain or achieve without sacrifice and hard work. We tend to be given a place, or we tend to make a place in this life based upon what we can afford for ourselves. My personal feeling is that I have never liked to be around people who see someone as a dollar. For instance, they treat someone who is known to have money as their best friend. Then they treat others who have a modest profession or make a modest income as second-class citizens. All this does for me is show me their values and also shows me that when it gets tough you can't rely on them because they are like the stock market. They can't handle the peaks and val-leys, the ebbs and flows of an unstable economy. They withdraw everything and hold tight. They withdraw from the investment. They withdraw and no longer give to the relationship. Don't ever expect to receive anything from them, and don't bother investing in them because their stability is based upon a volatile thought pattern and when it crashes, it crashes hard.

But what I really want you to understand in this section is that, just like taking care of yourself spiritually and physically, you need to see that when you make the investment and take care of yourself in all these areas that you keep them in order.

Then you don't have to worry about them. When areas of our lives are in order, there is peace about that area, and we can focus ourselves on areas that need more work and effort.

So it is with finances. Divorce statistics tell us that the number one reason for divorce is finance. If we don't define our finances, they will define us. If we don't limit our spending then our spending will limit us. It limits our options and opportunities. Paying off the past is constantly about having to look back and be reminded of bad decisions.

Being successful financially requires self-discipline, choosing to have fun by disciplining yourself financially. Seek financial counselors you can trust. I suggest you start with your spouse. I have been burned by bad financial advice, and I know I'm not alone. My advice is to go slowly, be wise, and don't do anything financially that you aren't comfortable with. Do your due diligence before making financial decisions. If you aren't comfortable, you will be spending precious mental, physical, emotional, and spiritual energy on something you probably shouldn't have done or wish you hadn't done. Very rarely, if ever, have I heard someone say something like, "I'm sure glad I did what I didn't want to do financially." So maintain control and discipline over your own finances. Create a financial and spending plan. Don't turn a blind eye towards them. Confront them, and be brutally honest in your assessment of them and make your finances work for you and not make yourself work for your finances. They will work for you. Smart, sound investing practices of a little over a long time reap huge rewards. Pay attention now, and don't lose hope. Gain confidence. We lose confidence by continually making bad decisions. Notice I didn't say bad mistakes. The word mistake to me insinuates no control. To me a mistake is two plus two equals five. You didn't decide to make it five instead of four. Decisions mean you have the control. You have thought through all the processes and made what seems to be the best decision you could have made given the circumstances.

I can write this from my own personal experiences. I have failed, and I have succeeded. I have prospered financially. I have used wisdom as well as been stupid in my dealings with finances, and I have paid a price. The greatest financial advice I can give anyone is to stay out of debt. Avoid the bad debt like a plague. Bad debt is credit cards. Good debt is an educational loan investing in your education. That's because a college education will pay off for you. But a credit card you have to pay off with interest. The education will give you a future, and bad debt will take away from your future.

> **h³** HOWARD'S HELPFUL HINT: *Alert! You may forfeit the future that could have been yours by making bad decisions financially.*

Financial

Goal: To be financially healthy and viable

Steps to attain Goal:

- Actively monitor my bank account balance.
- Develop a spending plan.
- Create a budget.
- Create investments and a savings plan.
- Get sound financial advice from someone I can trust.
- Make sure we are creating a future.
- Realize money is a tool not just a means to an end.
- Evaluate and reflect: measure my accomplishment by the use of a spreadsheet.

- Is my money working for me or me for it?

- Have I prepared for the unknown?

- What do I need to do differently?

- If married, are my spouse and I on the same page financially?

It's important to remember that your finances should work for you. Stay out of bad debt. That is credit card debt. A school loan isn't necessarily a bad debt because it gives you years of earning power you wouldn't have had.

Professional

Professionally investing in yourself is one of the greatest benefits you will ever reap. It is also the greatest thing you can do for your family. The profession you choose will determine your level of lifestyle, travel, income, and time. For instance, if I decide to become a professional, I know it will take a great investment of my time and money. But I also know it will reap a reward of great benefit of time, money, and lifestyle. However if I decide to not get an education and just do jobs that come to me, they are usually jobs no one else wants, then I have little to no investment and will reap little to modest income and live a reflective lifestyle.

What I have to realize is that it is my choice, no one else's. I need to seek those who can help me and mentor me, to get me where I want to go professionally. People who will invest a little time, encouragement, and advice are very helpful.

Once in my profession, I must invest in it just as I do in every other area of my life. If I neglect it and don't stay on top of my knowledge, then I lose ground professionally. Unfortunately, when people define themselves, they usually tell you what they do for a living–their profession. That seems to be their identity. However, I don't believe it is actually who they are. I think that is a very self-limiting description. I do, however, agree that you are what you are before you actually finish your degree. You know and see who you are or will become before you physically attain your degree.

Professional

- Goal: To invest and be the best professional I can be.

- Steps to attain that Goal:

- Prepare myself with education.

- Stay on top of current information about my profession.

- Find ways to earn promotion.

- Be active in my professional organizations.

- Evaluate and Reflect: Measure my accomplishments.

- Am I on a career track?

- Am I satisfied with the income and way of life it provides me?

- Am I improving yearly?

- What do I need to do differently?

- Am I still satisfied with my career choice?

- What do my peers and employers say about me?

It is important to realize that your profession is where you will spend the most of your time. Choose it wisely by choosing something you love to do. You have heard it said "Choose a career doing something you love and you will never work another day in your life." The truth is it will be work even though you may love it, but it won't seem laborious because it is your passion.

Rest and Recreation

I have to address this in today's world. Half the time, I don't know who is out playing and who is out working. Those working in business understand how intense the corporate world often is. They feel drained mentally and emotionally with nothing left to give at home or church or to their community. This area is so important. I like Steven Covey's approach in the book *The 7 Habits of Successful People.* Steven calls this principle "sharpening the saw." He states that you can return as a productive member of your family and society. I encourage you to read his book. I further encourage you to take his course. Steven knows you can't be at your best when you are dulled down by work and problems of everyday life. He encourages his readers to take time and sharpen their saw of life. He desires for you to be able to recharge your emotional and physical batteries, so to speak. I find that it seems we are pulled in every direction by well-meaning people only to return to work on Monday more tired than when we left on Friday.

The other extreme I see are those whom have the attitude that every day is a vacation and every day is a holiday and every meal is a feast. I see it in their approach to life and their profession. I am not talking about happy go lucky people here. I'm talking about people who think everything they do should be recreational. I want you to find that special thing in life that relaxes you. I loved the movie *Chariots of Fire.* The runner stated he felt God having pleasure in him running. I encourage you to find that recreational experience that you sense God has pleasure watching you enjoy it. It could be anything. I have a friend who works behind a desk forty or more hours a week. He finds working in the yard and gardening so refreshing. It is like it isn't even work for him. He loves being outside, listening to and watching the birds and animals. He even loves to mow the grass. Come to think of it, maybe he is nuts! Just joking. He gets his batteries recharged doing lawn work. That is relaxing to him. He finds that there is no one to talk back to him, no phone to have to answer, no one knocking on the door of his office with a deadline. It is just him and the outdoors, and he gets a tan in the process. He loves it. I actually like watching him because you can see the passion with which he gardens. For me, exercising recharges my batteries. Getting a massage monthly recharges me. Reading a book, spending time with family, and watching a movie recharges my batteries. So does a nice hot bath, with the door locked so that no one can enter my watery sanctuary. I apologize if that just gave you some kind of picture that only therapy will help get out of your head. So does sleep. I recommend we all get a little more sleep. It's okay. The world will be there when we wake up. Now design your recreational side of life to share in and recharge yourself in.

Recreational

- Goal: To enjoy my time off work and recharge my batteries.

- Steps to attain goal: Find a hobby I enjoy and can share with others.

- Make sure I take time to relax and rest.

- Create a hobby I can do alone or find alone time.

- Evaluate and Reflect: does my hobby actually drain/give me energy?

- Is my recreational activity a healthy one?

- Do I share it with others?

- Is it satisfying to my family and me?

Remember, it is important to find and do something you enjoy. Make it your own. It is okay if others think you are being a loner. You may need to schedule more alone time. Be creative. Have fun and recharge!

> **h³** HOWARD'S HELPFUL HINT: *Centered people prepare to be chosen in all areas of life.*

There is a scripture that says, "Many are called but few are chosen." Ever wonder why they aren't chosen. The most common place I see this is professionally. It's because they have not prepared themselves to be chosen. Do what it takes to stay on top professionally, just as you would in all the other areas we have discussed. This is placing yourself in a position to be successful. Give yourself the best chance possible to be successful. Don't get lazy and content. Enjoy it, but keep abreast of all the facts and prosper. Remember in Proverbs it says a little sleep, a little slumber, a little folding of the hands, and poverty will come upon you like a bandit. Laziness and slothfulness are active habits that will steal from you, in all areas of your life. You can't afford to get sloppy or lazy because the market and profession you are in is constantly changing. I'm a nurse. Trust me; nursing today isn't the same as when it was founded. However, if I choose to practice it the same as when Florence Nightingale discovered it, I would be in big trouble and I think Old Florence would be a little angry with me that I wasn't a better steward of my profession that she left for us.

> **h³** HOWARD'S HELPFUL HINT: *Work hard to become more than you are.*

I want people to want to become more than they ever thought they could. I want to help them reach that. I love seeing people actively involved in things larger than themselves. The trouble is I find myself wanting it for them more than they do. I find myself trying to make them want to be more. I found that I couldn't change people. Only you can change you. I can only give you the tools. What you do with them is up to you. Since I can't change people, I can at least inspire them. But, like the coach in the movie *Chariots of Fire* said, "I can't put in what God left out." I can't make you any more than you want to be if the gifts and tools to achieve it aren't inherent within you. We tend to become content when we experience measures of success. Then we maintain. Not me. I want to enjoy that success but I want to never stop growing so that I can move on to the next success.

I also find that when I don't pay attention to things I tend to get sloppy, a little slothful. I'm sure you can relate. Just go without washing or cleaning out your car for a little while and see the results. In the New Living Translation Bible, Proverbs 6:10–11 states, *"A little extra sleep a little more slumber, a little folding of the hands to rest-then poverty will pounce on you like a bandit; scarcity will attack you like an armed robber."* That is a sobering scripture. Become sloppy and slothful and lazy and the things you have worked so hard to attain will be stolen from you. None of it looks the same. You have to guard it. It steals what you worked so diligently to become. You can't sit still and stay the same.

I have had the privilege of attending many Boxing Hall of Fame induction weekends. I have met many fighters whom I admire because they continually paid the price and had the courage to attain their dreams. I have participated in races with them like a 5K and admired the fighter's humility and humanness. If you didn't know who they were, you wouldn't know they were famous. You can learn many lessons in life from these fighters.

One such lesson is that you can go from the headlines to the breadlines pretty quickly by not paying attention to the detail and staying on top of your profession. That's an old term to describe how fighters were taken advantage of by promoters and people around them. One day they are the newspaper headline, the big fight everyone wants to see. Then after it is over, they pay their bills and are left with little and even spending what they made thinking tomorrow would bring another headline fight. However, they often ended up with very little and found themselves begging for jobs and work, ending up in the breadlines. We have to stay on top of our business, both personal and professional, to avoid losing what we have worked so hard for.

22

SIN: Sickness in Nature

Oh wow, there he goes again with all that acronym stuff. Hey, it helps me remember. Anyway, I need to address an area of our lives that seems to destroy people. It breaks my heart to see people destroyed by SIN, whether it's a sin of omission or commission. I have seen careers, families, futures, and businesses all fail because of people's SIN. To me, sin is anything we know is morally or otherwise wrong that we give in to or choose to do regardless of knowing the right thing to do. We all read the newspaper headlines and were saddened to learn of former President Clinton as an example. President Clinton had arguably one of the best political minds we have known. However, his lifestyle showed that he committed immoral actions simply because he could. He admitted his actions were morally reprehensible. However, the damage was done to his career, his future, his family, and his reputation. He willingly inflicted pain upon others because of his own character flaws—his own selfishness, his own choices. We, too, must do whatever it takes to make sure we don't follow in those footsteps. I wonder how great a man he could have been had he disciplined his fleshly desires and placed that energy and time towards doing good.

We are all susceptible to this failure. That's the problem with having a sickness in our nature. It allows us the opportunity to do something that will kill us. I call it a sickness because I believe if we really knew the pain of the consequences we wouldn't do it. I do have to say, however, I have seen people who have known the pain and continue on without seeking treatment—alcoholics, addicts of all sorts, shopping, spending, talking, busybodies, cheaters, gamblers, sex. They all know the risks involved and make the choice to continue their behavior anyway. I am not saying they aren't trying to get help; I'm saying they haven't quite overcome it yet. And I'm not being judgmental. I have my faults to overcome as well. I'm in the medical profession. So let me give you a medical example. When you go to the doctor and he diagnoses you with a bacterial infection, you usually receive an antibiotic. Now this antibiotic is there to fight the sickness in your nature. There is a substance in your body that is foreign to you. In other words, it isn't natural to you and needs to be removed. It doesn't belong there; it's not in its normal state. It is in your body. The antibiotic fights the foreign substance in you causing your body to react differently than normal. The doctor gives you a ten-day supply of the antibiotic and tells you to take it till it's gone. Now what do you think will happen if you take it for only five days? You feel better, however, the sickness isn't totally gone even if you don't see signs of it. Chances are the infection is still there and can easily flare up again and make you sick unless you finish all the medicine prescribed. The tests the pharmaceutical companies performed tell us is that it takes ten days for that particular antibiotic to cure you by fighting off the infection. Oftentimes in some people they may need a different medication or more to fight off the sickness—hence my point when fighting off our sinful nature.

h³ HOWARD'S HELPFUL HINT: *We have to take the medicine as prescribed not as we want to.*

We can't consider the inconvenience of it; we have to con-sider the end result. Consider your desired result. I want healed of this nature, don't you? I want healed of anything that causes me failure or the chance to fail and harm others and myself in the process. I need to pay the price to get rid of the SIN: sick-ness in nature, so I can live abundantly. The scripture says, *"God sent his son so we may have life and have that life abundantly."* You can't have this way of life by serving a sin nature.

Kenneth Copeland reminds us to be *righteousness* conscious not *sin* conscious. I like that because it focuses our mind on the positive goal, reaching towards the upward call, forgetting the past, pressing on towards what's right, not what's convenient. I speak from personal examples as well. I'm human; I have my flaws. My wife can testify—I hope she won't (laughing)—that I am human and susceptible to failures. The problem with sin is that we usually get to do it in front of people so our failure is magnified. It has taken me years to overcome bad habits and things I'm not proud of because of my past, my childhood, and my nature. I allowed things in my life that weren't healthy to my body, soul, or mind. I failed, and I was responsible for allow-ing it to happen. I had a choice.

> h³   HOWARD'S HELPFUL HINT: *Centered people understand they make choices not mistakes.*

If you have stolen from another, it was a choice. If you add two plus two and get five, it's a mistake. I don't want to make it too simple, but that is how I see it. I am responsible for making the correct choices in life.

Things in my childhood that caused me to sin in anger, I couldn't have controlled. I was too young and didn't know or understand the affect those actions of others had on me, but I realized at a certain point in my life I had to take responsibility and choose to no longer use those things as an excuse, especially since I have been out of that environment longer than I was ever in it. I won't allow myself to be a victim, and I hope you decide the same. Take responsibility and use self-control and discipline.

I'm not underestimating the affect things like child abuse or alcoholism have had on a person. But I am saying it is important to recognize that they did have an affect on us and then deal with it in a healthy manner so we don't go on hurting others or ourselves. The scripture says that he who knows it's wrong and chooses to do it is in sin. I have heard others describe sin as temporary insanity. We don't know what we are doing; for if we did, we wouldn't do it. That's a tad extreme: however, there is a lot of truth in it. Dealing with sickness in our nature takes a commitment and assistance spiritually and sometimes from others as well. Psalm 119:3 (TLB), "*I have hidden your word in my heart that I might not sin against you.*" The writer of this Psalm is asking God to not let him sin, not let him give in to sin that may be lurking in his heart and causing damage to his relationship with God and others.

I want to encourage you. Our sinful nature isn't anything new to God. He isn't shocked when you sin. He is hurt and disappointed but only for your sake. He is there for you to grant you forgiveness and help. His love for us is so great. His word says in I Corinthians 2:9 (NLT), "*No eye has seen, no ear has heard, and no mind has imagined what God has prepared for those who love him.*" He has things for you to enjoy and do today, not just tomorrow or some distant time in space, but today!

God loves you so much that he sent his son, Jesus, to die on the cross take your sin nature upon him that you might live and not have to die as the hardened sinner you were destined to be. I don't know about you, but I couldn't give my son up for half this world. I don't have the love necessary to be able to do that. I'm so thankful God did. That's how much he loves us. I'm thankful I can let God be God. I can't do his job. Think about it just a bit. You know how much you love your children. You know the pain parents go through when they prematurely lose a child. Would you be willing to experience that? God *was,* and He *did* for you and me. He made a conscious decision for you and me. Let's not disappoint him by making sinful conscious decisions. Let's base our decisions on what he did for us on the cross.

Develop the spiritual part of your life to where you are so righteousness-focused that sin becomes a distraction to eliminate from your nature. You want to have a clean conscious and a clean mind and a spirit filled with pure thoughts and right desires. You need this purity so that you aren't soiled and dirtied by your contacts with the world and that you have instead created order and structure and are free to be deliberate and creative in all your dealings.

I don't want to set in motion things in my life that affect my family or others because of bad decisions based upon my choosing the easy way of sin. Strive at all costs to become strong, sinless, holy, blameless, guiltless, cleansed, restored, pure, devoted people, a people that are established, strong, immovable, completed, and secure in Christ Jesus. Be a blessing; by refusing the sin nature, you are placing yourself in a position for God to use you as a blessing to others. Then I believe your boundaries can be extended by the Lord farther beyond what you could actually believe, because he can trust you and knows you won't do harm to yourself as he moves you.

Again, I want you to know I don't write this chapter in arrogance and finger pointing. I write it from my own experience. After many failures, I have won most of my battles with sin, sickness, disease, double-mindedness, and self-destructive habits. Daily, I pay the price, take my medicine, and continue to overcome. I don't want to make it sound easy. It's not. I do want us all to recognize sin for what it is and choose to deal with it swiftly. Desire to remove it just as fast as if you were removing the flu from your body. I hope you will recognize that all men fall short of the glory of God. I John 1:8–9 (NLT) states, *"If we say we have no sin we are only fooling ourselves and refusing to accept the truth. But if we confess our sins [to Jesus], he can be depended on to forgive us and to cleanse us from every wrong."* Verse 10 goes on to say that if we say we have no sin, we are lying and calling God a liar for he says we have. A lot of people stop there. However, go ahead and keep reading. There is a remedy. John 2:1–2 basically states that Jesus is pleading with the Father for us because he took our sin upon himself, and he is the forgiveness for our sins. I don't judge people. We all are capable and susceptible of falling at any time. I don't care who you are. The scripture says there is forgiveness in Christ when you repent and receive it in faith. He judges the sin, not the sinner. He forgives you. He gives you an unlimited number of chances to always return to him. Let's choose to not practice those things we know are wrong. There are too many healthy things in life to concentrate on. Many great people in our history have fallen and stumbled in sin. Many of them got back up and dusted themselves off and made major contributions to this world in which we live. I trust after reading this you are inspired to do the same.

23

Commitment to Implementation

As you have been reading, to invest in yourself and others is a huge commitment to undertake. It takes a servant's heart and the road is rocky and full of holes, but I liken it a mountain climber. The climb takes preparation, stamina, desire, determination, courage, foresight, knowledge, skill, and trust. It takes the willingness to self-sacrifice, risking injury. All for the chance to see something few others ever get to see or experience. They pay the price. They reach their summit. They experience the joy of accomplishment. Then the reality also sets in. The descent can often be as dangerous as the ascent. They are just as careful, perhaps more so, in descending as they were in ascending. Their commitment to the implementation of all this is their pay off to safety and fulfillment. There are elements outside of their control that they have to carefully plan for and prepare for and deal with.

You, too, must have this same bull-dogged determination. You may not be ascending the highest physical mountains but let me assure you, you are ascending some of the highest spiritual, physical, mental, emotional, and financial mountains known to mankind. Your commitment to implementing your plan will be your determining factor for your success. I guarantee you rough roads ahead and falls and scrapes, but if you are willing to see those for what they are, setbacks and stumbles not permanent failures, then you will succeed.

> h³ HOWARD'S HELPFUL HINT: *Failures don't define us. They just humble us.*

Remember this is a journey to be experienced not a destination to drop out of life in. Investors never quit investing in themselves or others. That's their key to life and living and growth.

24

CENTERED PEOPLE ARE INVESTORS AND HAVE A STYLE OF GRACE

I love to watch true investors at work. They have developed a style of grace that gives to others without others feeling belittled. Those that they invest in feel like they have been to the auto shop and received a spiritual tune up. They recognize the willingness of the investor to give them time and effort. In my profession as a hospital administrator, I have multiple departments in a hospital that report to me. I notice that the workers always look at me to see if I am going to acknowledge them. They want to know I appreciate them and appreciate what they do. I can honestly tell you I do. I appreciate going into a clean bathroom, having a good hot meal, having lights and heat and air conditioning that work. I appreciate the efforts these people put out for my comfort. They invest in me and may not even know they are doing it. They think they just have a job. Not to me they don't. They are making daily investments. The truth is, I don't even know what half of them specifically do. I just appreciate the fact they are people and they are loved by a mother or family somewhere and are contributing as an investor for our comfort.

When you develop a style of grace people will sense it and want to be a part of it and have some of it rub off on them.

> **h³** HOWARD'S HELPFUL HINT: *Develop a style of grace.*

25

CENTERED PEOPLE HAVE LEARNED TO BECOME TEACHABLE

Being teachable is one skill you cannot go without and be successful to your fullest capabilities. I also like to refer to it as having a teachable spirit. You can probably picture people I'm talking about can't you? Of course none of us ever picture ourselves as being un-teachable. Kobe Bryant is being mentioned as having this attitude. His former coach, Phil Jackson, wrote in his book that Kobe would shake his head yes and then go out and not do what he had been instructed to do. He even shook his head yes and told his coach he understood what he was supposed to do and then chose to do something different. It ultimately cost his team the overall title one year. Sure his team had success, but it was limited by attitudes of not being teachable or coachable. One may be able to have different measures of success without being teachable, but that person is rare. That person is being allowed to be un-teachable probably for different reasons, such as inheriting the family business, and no one cares about being teachable if an employer is allowing it to take place. You see this with many athletes who are naturally gifted but won't listen to their coach or teammates. But trust me when I say that their success will never reach its fullest potential because they will cap themselves off by being un-teachable. If I ever get that way I hope someone likes me enough to pull me aside and tell me what I need to hear, not what I may want to hear.

Today, the younger generation complains and says, "I just got lectured" or "Please don't lecture me," even for the smallest of things. That is an attitude of being un-teachable. It will ultimately cost them. A lesson in what a "lecture" truly is is in order for them. The lectures I received I usually deserved or paid for. I usually got it for performing badly by a coach, or I paid for it by going to college and learning.

You notice people who are teachable. They look at their teachers with intensity in their eyes and their ears perking with attentiveness to every word. They act like if they miss anything being said they will fail the exam or session. They listen with an intensity that suggests life itself hangs in the balance. They listen that way because they know if they miss something it may ultimately cost them what they have worked so hard to attain for themselves or their team. I love the focus that teachable people have developed.

I remember listening to an interview with a person in Clinton's cabinet during his first term. That person, who refused to be identified, said that during a debate of important issues the president was talking about other issues and was told by the vice president that he needed to get his head cut in and quit the other talk. In public, the president never let on like that may have bothered him. We also don't know what was said later behind closed doors. It might not have bothered him because we all need people in our lives to help us in this area. This also shows you no matter what level you are on you will always need the skill and focus of being teachable.

26

ACCEPTING CRITICISM:
A BADGE OF HONOR

Being teachable requires this next skill—accepting criticism. Centered people have trained themselves to do this with grace and style. You know I mentioned earlier how much I liked the Proverbs. Proverbs tells us how to deal with this as well. Proverbs 23:12 (TLB) says, *"Don't refuse to accept criticism, Get all the help [knowledge] you can."* I often admire people who accept criticism and don't take things personally. Look at Proverb 25:12 (TLB). It says, *"It is a badge of honor to accept valid criticism."* What, a badge of honor? How about a badge of embarrassment? Why does it say that in the Proverbs, the book of wisdom? I will tell you. It is because only a fool believes everything he does is so great and worthy of praise. It's not always the criticism that bothers me, but it's the tone one uses in addressing me in front of others that may be the cause of me not readily accepting criticism. Also it is an act of kindness when one gets valid criticism because it shows me that person actually cares for me. I have found that most of the time when people don't like me, they usually just leave me alone or criticize me in a negative way. When people like me, they tease me and rough me up a bit. They could move on to others, but they don't. It's because they like me. That's not a bad thing. Most of us take things so personally that we can't accept it when someone points out a fault or criticizes us.

> **HOWARD'S HELPFUL HINT:** *Accepting criticism isn't a final judgment of who you are. It's a critique of a certain point in time.*

That's it. Don't make it more than that. You aren't being defined by it. You aren't destined to failure because someone criticized your performance, your hair, or your attitude. Psalm 141:5 (TLB) states, *"Let the Godly smite, [correct] me! It will be a kindness! If they reprove me it is medicine! Don't let me refuse it."* Criticism and correction is an act that can be taken as a blessing. My son received a speeding ticket. He was angry when he went to church and heard the youth pastor state that he too was pulled over by a policeman for speeding but didn't get a ticket. He asked me why God let the pastor off and not him? I said to him to look at it from another perspective. Perhaps God did let him off and actually allowed Zach to be pulled over to get his attention that in his speeding and not paying attention, he could hit a kid who might run out in the street chasing a ball or riding a bike.

Zach said, "Oh, okay." I told him the laws are there to protect us not restrict us. It was a good corrective lesson he took to heart. I'm proud of his mature response as a seventeen-year-old.

> **HOWARD'S HELPFUL HINT:** *Sometimes what appears as God's judgment against us is actually his mercy saving us from harm.*

Take the reality show *American Idol*. Those contestants pour their souls into their performance only to be hacked down by a critic. If they have learned to listen, then they pick out the gold nuggets and use them to perform better next time. If they take it personally, as I have witnessed, they lash back with a snide comment of their own. Olympic athletes in gymnastics experience the same thing. It's a subjective judgment. At times, we pour so much of ourselves into someone or something that it is really hard to not take things personally. I can attest to that.

When I trained and ran marathons, I had some runners tell me that I would never get better than my original time. They based this on performances I turned in. Now I could have tucked my tail in and run and cursed them, but I didn't. I also didn't let their criticism determine how fast I would run or how well I would perform. That is because I was running for me not them. And by the way, I did turn in better times later on. They critiqued me not knowing all the facts, such as if I had the proper amount of training while juggling a family and a career. They didn't know that sometimes it was all I could do to even get to a race. No matter. It didn't define me and guess what. It won't define you either. I ended up running twelve marathons and multiple other races. I ran two marathons in one week with a friend of mine, Kevin Bocquin. I don't recommend that, but I guarantee you not many have done that.

> h³ HOWARD'S HELPFUL HINT: *Remember to never let the success or the failure define you.*

The box people place us in to define our success and failure is too small for any of us. Proverbs 15:31–32 (TLB) states, *"If you profit from constructive criticism you will be elected to the wise men's hall of fame. But to reject criticism is to harm yourself and your own best interests.*" How about that? Accepting criticism places you in some prestigious company. Sometimes we need criticism and correction. Don't ever be so arrogant you can't receive it from someone. You want to know how I got over taking criticism personally?

I Started Asking for It

Sometimes onlookers see things we don't. This is often because we are too close to the situation. Take football fans criticizing the quarterback. We see things he didn't because we have a different perspective. We have an overview. He is in the middle of that field without the luxury of our overview. It's the same thing. It's odd how many people criticize without ever entering into the field of play or arena of work isn't it? That's okay. Let them be who they choose to be, our shoulders are large enough to carry it. You and I will dare to dream big, fail big, succeed big, and live big. The quarterback didn't allow his critics to determine if he would play again. You and I have no business giving any critic that amount of power in our lives. It's just their perspective and may be right or wrong. Bring it on! I will use it as a learning tool not a life-defining tool. I may be able to use some of it to help me succeed, and I can discard the rest of it. Remember, don't take it personally.

Change your Perspective

Be quick to listen and slow to get angry. James 1:19–20 (NLT) states, "*Understand this, my dear brothers and sisters. You must all be quick to listen, slow to speak, and slow to get angry. Human anger does not produce the righteousness God desires.*" Good advice. Change your perspective from "taking things personally" to "I want to improve and get better." Be done with anger. Then growth will come. Your eyes are no longer on you but on your performance. See the difference? One is personal and one is objective.

27

CENTERED PEOPLE DEVELOP TEMPERAMENT

I can't tell you how many times I have run into someone who considers himself a professional; yet, he has not developed the temperament for his job. It's kind of like seeing a mother who loves but yet yells at her children whenever they fail or spill milk. Develop the temperament you need for the role you play in your family, on your professional team, and in society. God also will temper you in life as he molds and shapes you into the person you and he desire.

I have been in corporate meetings and military meetings and witnessed people who allowed themselves to scream and act unprofessionally. It was embarrassing to see grown people act that way. As mentioned earlier, two-year-old little kids can yell and throw temper tantrums. Look at Proverbs 15:18 (TLB), *"A quick tempered man starts fights, a cool tempered man tries to stop them."* Ever heard the saying "cooler heads prevailed"? That's because the cooler heads had developed temperament. They disciplined their emotions and chose temperament. It doesn't mean they didn't care or weren't angry. They just learned to temper their behavior and actions.

You really have to know yourself to make this successful. I found that my wife is a wonderful schoolteacher. She looks for ways to help children learn and help them through their struggles. On the other hand, I myself am not nor could I be a good schoolteacher. I don't have the temperament or the patience. My attitude is hey if you can't get it then you aren't trying hard enough. That wouldn't make me successful in a high school setting would it? I haven't developed the temperament necessary for teaching school as a profession. However, it does help me as an emergency department nurse. When things are bad and patients are traumatized with injuries, you have to think fast and quick and respond instantly or life may stop, as they know it. I can do that. I have learned the temperament of handling that pressure by using critical thinking skills. My wife learned her temperament through caring as well. I learned early in life, I can raise two children just not thirty of them in a classroom. That's knowing yourself, your situation, and developing the temperament it takes to be successful. You have to actively choose this. Not passively. The temperament won't just fall on you. You must develop it. I developed it by deciding I wouldn't panic in traumatic situations. I learned to keep my cool, think critically and responsively, and act appropriately. Not so hard—I just made the choice to do it. I have witnessed physicians who should be held in high esteem because of their medical knowledge and skills, only to be embarrassed to watch them lower their status in people's eyes because of a lack of temperament and poor bedside manner. How many professional athletes have we seen do the same thing? Yell and scream because the referee made a mistake or because they made a mistake. Half the time, it looks idiotic to say the least. Don't let that be you.

28

FROM HUMBLE AND ANGRY
BEGINNINGS TO A THANKFUL HEART

When I was young and my father was killed in Vietnam, I was angry. I wanted to hurt anyone who looked Vietnamese. After all, I could justify it. One of theirs killed one of mine. I grew up hurting people just to watch them hurt. Earliest I can remember doing this was when I was eight years old. I would cowardly do it and stand back and laugh. That's how hurt I was. I would justify it by saying that someone hurt me so now someone must pay. The rock group, The Eagles, has a song that says "Anger is just love disappointed." I have to agree with that. I was hurt that something I loved was taken from me, and I let it make me angry. Then I carried that anger out in a wrong, unhealthy way. I am so thankful that God never let go of me. If it weren't for his grace, I would have done some really regrettable things. My mom had remarried, and I didn't exactly get along with my step-dad. However, today we have a good relationship. At seventeen, I joined the military and had to sacrifice and learn new ways of life. No drill sergeant was there to tell me how much he loved me. At least I don't think it was love I heard through all of his yelling.

h³ Howard's Helpful Hint: *Centered people wisely accept course corrections.*

At that time, another course correction came my way. I had dropped out of high school and ended up getting caught in the military without a diploma, so they took me out of the school I was in and made me study to pass the GED. Let me tell you, staying in school would have been easier. That was a difficult test. To make matters funny, I was in intelligence school in Fort Huachuca, Arizona, and I flunked out. That's right, I am actually a guy who flunked out of intelligence school. Now I will be the running joke at your dinner party. Ha, Ha, Ha. It wasn't for lack of intellect or I never would have gotten into the school. It was because it bored me, and I didn't like it so I didn't put forth any effort. That's not even the funny part. When I flunked out and since my entrance test scores were so good, they sent me off to Nuclear Weapons School and I became a Nuclear Weapons Specialist with hours earned towards a degree in Rocket Science at the University of Alabama-Huntsville. Now that's funny. Upon arrival to the technical school, I had absolutely no confidence, and I was wondering what the army was thinking. I just flunked out of intelligence school and now I have to work on warheads? Can things actually get any worse for me? Certain failure looms ahead, I feared. Even I know something about this isn't right. We will all be killed. I can't do this. We were taken to the specialist school in which had a sign above the doors that read "Through these doors pass the best technicians in the world." I felt that pain in the pit of my stomach. Certain failure. I couldn't even spell technician, let alone become one. But God knew me and knew what I needed and again put me around some Christians who helped me gain confidence and gave me some love. I did pass school. It was then that I was sent to Germany, where I performed maintenance on nuclear warheads. I was stationed in Northern Germany in a NATO unit with the British, Scottish, and Irish militaries. I had a great time and even flew air missions with the British Royal Air Force. Even at eighteen, I knew that was a special time. I had a crypto clearance, which is higher than a top-secret clearance. Oh the stories I could tell you. But I won't.

In Germany, I was without much money, constantly hungry, and skinny. I was angry, and I ran a lot and became one of the better runners on our base. Only one person there could consistently beat me at long distance. He was a natural long distance runner; I had to work at it. No one was there to hold and love me and there was no one to share Thanksgiving and Christmas with. I had people feel sorry for me and "invite a soldier over" for the holidays. I am thankful that I didn't have to spend it alone; however, you understand, it still wasn't with family. I had a void in my heart and life that God was trying to fill if only I would let him. I was a loner. I didn't like people much since all they ever did in my eyes was criticize me or knock me around. I constantly replayed the negative things people had done and said to me. I would go out to nightclubs in Germany by myself. I wasn't afraid to die. I'm not bragging. I'm saying that's how hard I had become at such a young age. I couldn't speak the language, nor did I know anyone, but that didn't matter. I had me. Drugs and alcohol did abound, though I participated very little in the drugs. I did do my share of alcohol. Terrorists were there too. I didn't participate with them either. We just hung out in the same clubs. We danced liked no one else until they would make us leave the clubs. "Too bad for these people" was my attitude. Don't mess with me. Subconsciously, I thought people were just here to hurt me. At times, I would hurt people just because I was so angry. I believed people weren't beings to love; they were to be conquered. But thank God for his love!

Since I had recently become a Christian, God was working on my heart and my destiny. He never left me, and I believe saved me out of harm's way many times. It's funny that even when you are blind and think you are big and bad and tough, there are always bigger, worse, and tougher people. It didn't matter to me how big they were, I still would stand and give it a go. I learned that I may lose the fight, but they are going to get hurt in the process.

On God's faithfulness and protection to me, one time I was lost, I didn't speak the language, and this man walks up to me and I ask him for directions. He spoke perfect English. We were on a road that you could see for a quarter mile or more. I walked about a hundred yards and turned around, and he was gone. It dawned on me that he spoke to me first in English and spoke it without a German accent. I am convinced to this day he was an angel of the Lord. God sends what we need when we need it. I am so thankful he didn't let me stay the way I was. God loved me to who I am today. He loved me when I wasn't loveable. He knew why I wasn't loveable or capable of giving love. He knew that, at times, men act tough out of fear. Yet that didn't stop him. He sent people my way at the right times to chisel off the cold stone I had let my heart become. He helped me to soften my spirit.

I was attending church and listening to a man of God named Derek Prince, who would say how much God loved us and had a future for us and could change us. I also heard Derek, on several occasions, state how God had "severely" dealt with him personally on some issues. He knew a God who severely dealt with him because he knew that God loved him, and he trusted God. Listening to Derek, you would have thought he and God were always looking at each other physically. That is how well Derek knew the Lord. Wow, was I ever shocked. I had hurt my elbow using nun chukkas, a Chinese martial arts weapon. Derek prayed for me and my elbow was instantly healed. That is when the real revelation of God's love for me came through. I had always heard about people being healed; however, I wasn't quite sure about it. Now I had experienced it. God met me where I was and gave me a gift—his healing. All I gave him was my thanks and an injured body. What a deal that turned out to be. That's how much God loves us.

29

Becoming a Christian

My sophomore year of high school, I was in the locker room after football practice and one of the star players said he was going to the revival that one of the local churches was sponsoring. I looked up to him as a good athlete, and I asked why he was going. He told me he thought it would do him some good. He was tough so I said, "Okay, I will go too since most of the town will be there."

Weeks before, I worked for a trash hauler who scared the lights out me. He looked at me and pointed at a highway overpass and said "You know if I ran into that and killed myself I would go to heaven. Would you?"

Well I thought, you know this guy is half nuts enough to do this. So sheepishly I said, "I don't know."

He then told me about God. He said he would look for me at the revival. I thought *yeah, right*. Alice Cooper was my God at the time. So after the jock said that he was going, I showed up. And yes, there was the trash hauler, a local deacon of the church all dressed up.

> h³   HOWARD'S HELPFUL HINT: *God will use people to get you where he wants you.*

The evangelist preached on hell and scared me right in to Christianity. I went forward and accepted Jesus Christ as my Lord. I went all week because each night the evangelist would say something different I hadn't done or something wrong I had done. I went forward every night that week. That's how dumb and scared I was. I was covering all my bases. Asking Christ once was enough, but what did I know. I do have to make this point.

My life was such a mess that Jesus took hold of me and hasn't let go since. It wasn't just religion. I actually felt different and noticed a difference. I learned God was actually alive. I couldn't believe someone actually loved me enough to die for me and give me a good life. Christianity is a relationship with the Lord. It is a lifelong commitment and process. It isn't playing church and holding on to the rulebook. It is having a vibrant, active relationship with the God who created this universe and everything in it. I learned God loved me so much he was after me from an early age. I saw things spiritually, but just felt like I was a nut or hallucinating. It turns out I wasn't. Satan was trying to keep me from asking the Lord into my life. I am convinced if I had rejected the Lord I wouldn't be alive today. I was an extreme person. I didn't do a little alcohol. I did a lot. I smoked a lot. I did all the wrong stuff a lot. I was a "type A" personality out to prove myself worthy to the world. So my life took off from there. And it hasn't been boring.

HOWARD'S HELPFUL HINT: *Centered People know that God has an amazing life for them as well.*

30

As I Centered Myself,
I Learned to Forgive

I was extremely bitter yet a fairly optimistic person. I learned to forgive over a period of time. I learned that God had forgiven me and that I couldn't earn his love or forgiveness. I also learned that the Lord's Prayer said to forgive us as we forgive those who trespass against us. I was in a quandary. I couldn't be forgiven unless I forgave others. There was no way out of that one. I lived in Germany one full year before returning to the USA and seeing my family. Over that year, I prayed a lot and expressed a lot of anger to God, and he gave me the ability to forgive all those who had hurt me. Yes, it took nearly the full year to forgive and get healed of the anger I had carried like an old friend. Like I mentioned earlier, it is a process not a one-time event. As the scripture states, he who is set free is free indeed. That was who I was becoming, a free man. A man freed from anger, resentment, and hurts caused from a painful past.

> **h³** HOWARD'S HELPFUL HINT: *Centered people know forgiveness is the key to freedom.*

You are probably wondering how in the world one could overcome these obstacles and challenges and not be bitter. I like the movie *Oh Brother Where Art Thou?* They are uneducated hicks trying to make a better life in this world for themselves the only way they know how, only to be always bumbling along the way. In one part it was said that they would encounter many obstacles on their way to the treasure they were seeking. That is so true in life. If we overcome the obstacles, we will get our treasures. I also often find my treasures looking different than what I thought they might. I found what I truly treasured wasn't material things or revenge; it was people.

Earlier I stated we aren't victims. Even if I have been wronged or victimized, it doesn't mean I have to walk around with the spirit of being a victim. I made a decision to forgive. I forgave people who had hurt me, and I even forgave God. You ask, forgave God? Yes. God doesn't sin, however I was bitter at him for allowing things in my life that I thought he could control. I have learned later that God isn't necessarily involved in everything that happens to us. Trust me, God is big enough to handle our ignorance. When I forgave, I found that all that was binding me released. It was one of the best moves I ever made. I no longer had to carry that old, filthy baggage of hatred and resentment that was taking up so much room in my heart that I hadn't any room for love. I no longer wanted to hurt or avoid people. It was then that I left the life of a loner behind. I remember walking to my barracks and realizing God didn't desire for me to be a loner. It was a revelation for me as a young man using any protective defense mechanisms possible to survive emotionally.

The miracle was when I returned from Germany after that year of being away. My family saw me differently and I saw them differently. I think it was because I was looking through different eyes this time. I had become different. I had grown.

Parts of my past were left behind for good. I was friendlier. I was in great physical shape (and much more handsome if I do have to say so myself). I was also in the best spiritual shape I had ever been in. It wasn't an easy process, and it didn't happen overnight. In fact, a lot of times it was very painful. But those times did pass. I would forgive people only to have the next week something remind me of what they did to me, and the process kept repeating itself until finally I had enough breakthrough that it became easier to forgive. I also strongly suggest you do the old adage. "Forgive and forget." I could understand people better and realize they were people like me who hurt just as much as I did and that's what caused them hurt me.

Remember Jesus' words on the cross? Luke 23:34 (NLT) states, *"Father, forgive them for they don't know what they are doing."* Wow! I lived that because as we hurt each other I don't think we really know what we are doing, or we probably wouldn't do it.

In one emergency department where I worked, there was a baby two months old that had been abused. That's right, two months old not two years old. Some of my colleagues said, "Don't you just want to kill the man who did that." They pointed at him; I saw that he was standing over to my right. It was the baby's father. He and I locked eyes for a moment. I was shocked by my own response. I stated, "How hurt or sick must a person be to do that to another person." I actually understood this offender's pain. I looked at him and saw the fear in his eyes. I couldn't cast judgment on him because I knew he needed so much help. I don't know what happened to him after all that, but the lesson I took away was that we are living in a society and world of hurt and wounded people who desperately need help and need God. I know God loves that man. I also know God despises the sin and hurt he caused. The lesson is God hates the sin but loves the sinner. That doesn't mean you get away with sin. There are consequences. These people are wealthy and poor alike. Hurts don't discriminate by your income or lifestyle. I often find myself praying quietly when I see children abused or being scolded in public. I pray God will send someone their way so that they may be healed and learn of his love for them. Otherwise, the cycle of hurt and pain never ends.

31

GOD: A FATHER TO THE FATHERLESS

So you see after that portion of my life, I figured it could only get better. I have always been optimistic. Glass is half full, not half empty kind of guy. That is not to say I don't experience times of wanting to throw in the towel. But at that time I was so far down it couldn't get worse. To this day, I thank God daily for the life he has given me. In Psalms 68 it says, *"I will be a father for the fatherless."*

John and Kathy Brown, who were my first high school Sunday school teachers, were people who invested in me and taught me that scripture. I am ever so thankful for people like John and Kathy. They lay their lives down for others. I was like—wow can God possibly even want to be my dad? That's a fantasy, isn't it? It took a while to sink in, but today I realized that I could have no better father than God himself. I also learned that he gave me an inherent ability to believe in the unseen and have a faith I don't see others have. I'm not saying that arrogantly or like I am so special. I was so far down in life that believing in God was actually easy for me. God was either going to pull through, or I was a history. I believe God knew me before I was born and knew what I would go through and knew the extra amount of faith it would take for me to make it through life.

HOWARD'S HELPFUL HINT: *Centered people know that God pursues us! God pursued me, and he is still pursuing you.*

Think about that for a moment. The God who created everything you see is pursuing you. I suggest you find out what he wants and do it. You may think he isn't pursuing you. I suggest you just learn to listen for him. You will find him if you do. Because God pursued me, I am now a man of faith instead of a case study in criminal behavior.

32

DEVELOP A TIMELINE

Develop a timeline of your life. Really, do it now. Lay the book down and do it. I think you will be amazed as you compare where you began to where you are now and realize the faithfulness of God that it took to get you there. Don't place every little detail in this, but look at the measures of success you have had. I think you will be amazed. I know I am. Do it and let your heart become thankful.

33

LIVE A LIFE OF FAITH AND ADVENTURE

I was eating lunch one afternoon with my brother-in-law. It was snowing, and I said. "Ed, I miss living by faith. I miss the sense of adventure and hope I once had."

As Ed often did, he listened without judging and said, "Yes, I know what you mean."

I said, "We have cars, a house, kids, jobs, and status quo lives. I want more than that." I was saying that didn't take much faith for me to have. At one point in my life it might have, but not at this time—turns out that God was placing on my heart the desire to become more in him.

I often wonder why people settle for status quo. I'm not being judgmental. Adventures aren't for everyone. In my life, I can't sit still. Status quo for me is like locking a lion in a cage where he is no longer able to roam the range and be king. My eyes would be rolling back in my head. It's just not for me. We are all wired a little differently; I'm just sharing with you how I'm wired. So I decided to look for a new job. I probably could have resisted and told the Lord no, but then I would have missed out on all he had for me to experience. I would have missed out on his best for me.

The Garth Brooks song "The Dance" says it so eloquently, "*I could have missed the pain, but I would have had to miss the dance.*" I have learned that the pain never lasts and isn't equal to the joy of victory in life. The pain is worth the price. I believe Jesus would say that too since he went through the ultimate pain and paid the price to be seated at the right hand of the Father.

It was a difficult decision, but I was experiencing unrest in my life and knew it wasn't a midlife crisis. I had worked for a great healthcare company named Heartland Health for nineteen years. I worked with great people, but still I just felt it was time to do something different, even if it meant leaving behind years of building I had done. It's so important for you to understand the sense of timing I am speaking of. I then began the process of preparing my family for a move out of our comfort zone and towards a life of adventure. I ended up interviewing at seven places, being offered jobs at more than half, but I never felt them to be the right thing in my heart. It was irritating too. I had coworkers saying I was being too picky. I was just kicking tires and not really going to buy the car so to speak. I had recruiters lie behind my back about me. It wasn't pleasant. I was discouraged and felt at some point in my life I had probably sinned beyond repair or that God couldn't possibly use me for anything good in this life.

Finally, I went to interview in Salina, Kansas, in August of 1999. I was praying as I drove, and as I pulled up to my hotel on that hot 103-degree Sunday afternoon, I asked God if this was the place. My spirit witnessed it wasn't. I got a tad angry and said to God, "Why would you have me drive all this way only to tell me when I get here it's not the right place. You could have told me at home." I will never forget what God impressed upon me at that time.

In his love and mercy he said, "Yes I could have told you, but you would be wondering if you really heard me or not. You need to come and see for yourself that this is not what I have for you." Instead of wondering did I really hear God or was that just a voice of fear from me because I really didn't want to go. Well, I went the next day to my interviews and about three hours into it, the CEO and COO said, "You are way overqualified for what we are looking for. We don't think you would be happy here and this is really not what you are looking for as well." I said that I agreed, we shook hands, and I left. They were really good people. They were gentle and nice about it, and stated that they too had been in my shoes and then told me to keep the faith.

> **h³** HOWARD'S HELPFUL HINT: *It's so important to learn to hear and discern the leading of God.*

It was a hard experience for me. It takes faith and a realization that even if you miss it, God can correct it all for you. A lesson I couldn't have learned any better.

I Found Home away from Home

I sat at dinner with my wife and kids and I said, "Kids we are going to move. I'm taking my career to another level. We will live anywhere but California or New York." I didn't know God was listening. That next week, I had an offer to fly to New York and interview at Upstate University Hospital in Syracuse. It was actually one or two levels higher as a VP than my resume or experience showed. The recruiter said he had five candidates. I hated flying so the day before I left to interview I called him and said, "I can't possibly stand a chance. How about I back out?"

He said, "I think you have a great chance." So I couldn't wiggle out of it. I flew to New York. Got off the plane, went outside of the airport, and felt in my spirit like I was home. I felt comfortable. This feeling was unlike all the others I had experienced. I then relaxed knowing, after all I had gone through with God, that this was going to work out. I was actually walking around the campus and praying. I said, "God could you possibly have this much for me?" I actually didn't believe God could have so much more for me than what I thought possible. That's how much he loves us. It turns out, they had better qualified candidates on paper but none that fit like I did. To make a long story short, it worked out great. I left with a resume second to none and plenty of experiences to last a lifetime and great people with whom I spent time. Like the book said, it was the best of times it was the worst of times. My kids didn't want to leave their friends and home, but now they are so thankful they did. My wife got her master's degree paid for and is graduating from Syracuse University. We were blessed to be a part of this great central New York community. We also attended a great church, Abundant Life Christian Center, that is doing mighty things for the region and the world, pastored by Senior Pastors John and Lisa Carter. Wonderful things are happening through their ministry. New York City gives the rest of the state a bad name. Upstate New York is filled with great people. They also tolerate a lot, and I mean a lot, of snow. At times, I felt like I lived in a snow globe. The people are guarded, but I have come to love them. I wouldn't trade my time here for anything in the world. I also can't wait to see the next new adventure God has planned for my family and me.

One of the biggest reasons for the move, I realized, is that God not only had plans for me but for my family as well. It was a tremendous decision that came at a price. I knew it could determine whom my kids marry and where they spend the rest of their lives. They would no longer call Missouri home. As hard as that is, it is still better to leave your children's future in God's hands and be there for them. That's what this book is all about, investing in their lives and my life and others lives and growing into more than I had ever dreamed possible.

> **h³** HOWARD'S HELPFUL HINT: *Develop a sense of timing.*

Developing a sense of timing means knowing when to make the moves you need to make. I was playing in a high school football game. We had driven downfield and were about to score. On this play, my role was to block the defensive end completely out of the play. I did, and we scored. However, I didn't hear the ref blow the whistle, and I kept blocking this guy. The ref ran over and grabbed me by the shoulder pads and stated, "Hey stop; you scored. It's over." I turned and joined the celebration. As I look back, I have seen times in my life when I kept fighting professionally or personally only to realize that the fight was already over. I was the only one still fighting.

> **h³** HOWARD'S HELPFUL HINT: *Centered people realize when it's time to move on.*

You can still continue to fight through it and have people look at you like you have lost your mind and you can make it feel like a slow amputation, where by the time its over, everyone is glad to see you leave or cut off from the organization or relationship. I prefer the other option of keeping my intuition based on a sense of timing and discernment and quit fighting and move on in a healthy manner.

What do I mean by this? I learned that to be a servant and to love people, you have to be there when others can't or won't be. You need to love them when they are at their best and worst.

Adding Brenda and her family to my life was such a distinct blessing from God. The scripture says he who finds a wife has found favor with God. Amen to that. I have learned so much from her steadfastness and love. Her commitment to God, family, and me are second to none. It's hard being married to a man of faith who does things when others can't see why he would do them. She comes from a great farm family of eight kids.

I always get a kick out of listening to her father's fishing stories. He and his buddies were sitting outside on his eightieth birthday and telling these stories. Then, all of the sudden, they started correcting each other. They had told those stories so many times the details blurred and everyone, including myself, felt like we had caught the fish. They are a great family to be a part of.

34

TRAGEDY STRIKES A LOVING FAMILY

It was early April 1986, when my close brother-in-law, Ed Simpson, knocked on my door at lunchtime. Ed and I married twin sisters. He told me that Brenda's brother, Johnny, had been found dead along the road after a one-car crash. I now had to break this news to my wife—she had lost a brother in a car accident. I wish that chore on no one. However, when I became an emergency department nurse I did have the unenviable task of doing it multiple times for other families. It hurts to give that news to anybody. I remember when we were getting ready to go to the funeral; Brenda yelled at me to go get my father-in-law because we were running late. He was still upstairs in his bedroom. This man never met someone he didn't give a chance to or welcome, no matter what past you had. I always admired that about him and my mother in law. So anyway, I was like, "Why isn't he in the car yet?" I went up the stairs to get him, and he was devastated. I had never seen him in this state of mind before. It was all he could do to stand on two feet. I helped him straighten his tie and I said, "C'mon, George, we need to go now."

He said, "This is the worst day of my life. No one should ever have to do this…bury my own son. I can't do this." I told him I would be with him and took this strong, courageous man by the hand and steadied him as we walked to the car.

> h³ HOWARD'S HELPFUL HINT: *Be there for people when others choose not to be.*

My heart was overwhelmed. I cried like a baby at the funeral. I cried as much for George and Mary Lou and their pain as I did for our loss. It wasn't a job or task I had volunteered for, but I was probably the best one for it at that time. God is like that. He will use you when you think you shouldn't be used. I was able to express to my in-laws the true love in my heart for them. The next day, my mother-in-law was out in her garden. I hugged her and asked, of course as a lame idiot, "How are you?"

She looked in my eyes and said "I could just die." Her heart, like my heart, was broken, and she grieved like it was not repairable. A part of me realized that a part of her and George did die that day with her son. Sure they had seven children to lean on, but each one of them was equally important in memory and love as the next. Nothing could ever replace their son, John, in their lives, nor should anything. There is a feeling of closeness that follows the death of a loved one in a family. All too often, as in our family, that feeling and closeness with all the members of the family only lasts for a period of time. I wish it had lasted longer. I accept my role in it not lasting longer as well. A life lesson learned through experience.

35

Getting Accepted into the Family

Before I asked Brenda to marry me, I asked her father if it would be okay. He stated in the fashion of the man he is and looking at me like I was an idiot for asking him, "What does she think of the idea?"

I said, "I think she likes it."

He said, "Well then, there you go." So I walked off with my tail between my legs wondering what I'd done or if I had just been threatened. When I asked Brenda to marry me, she said yes. The next day we went to spread the news to our folks. Brenda said "Hey, Mom, see my ring."

Her mom looked at the engagement ring with one eye and the other eye glaring up at me and said, "Oh how nice, a friendship ring."

I didn't even know that was physically possible to do that with your eyes. I, of course, proceeded to run like a little girl to the next room, leaving my future bride to fend that one on her own. It wasn't one of my proudest moments.

After several hours of sitting in silence except for the football game on TV, my future mother-in-law said "Well, Howard, we welcome you to the family," and gave me a hug. I almost felt like it was the hug of the mafia. You know, the one that says, "Kill the one I hug."

I was like, "Yeah right! God, don't let my feet fail me now." I don't know if my feet touched the ground on the way to the car. It was a while before any of them took to me I think. Brenda's twin sister's response upon learning of the engagement, yelled at me. Linda said, "What did you do to my sister?" I can still see her in my mind today saying it as if it were yesterday. I still don't know why I didn't turn around and run. I guess I wasn't smart enough to, but I'm glad I didn't. That day I became part of a real family. Come to think of it, now I understand why I enjoyed running so much. I became good at it out of necessity.

36

GOD ACCEPTS AND MEETS US WHERE WE ARE

God is so loving and a comedian too. I bet he was laughing and having a field day watching me work my magic in fear. Just like my wife's family saying welcome to the family, God says it too. Welcome to the family just as you are. They all took me for who I was, not who I was going to become.

> **h³** HOWARD'S HELPFUL HINT: *Accept people for who they are, not what they have.*

Of course, I bet my mother-in-law became very spiritual and prayed a lot before I married her daughter. I probably owe her because some of my unknown success is due to her prayers. Oh yeah, I forgot to tell you when we got engaged, I had 400 dollars to my name and was just fresh out of the military with no real job. I didn't even own a car. No wonder they thought we were nuts. Years later, when I asked my mother-in-law what she thought she said, "I knew you were fresh out of the military and it might be hard for a while but that you would do well." I appreciate that confidence she had in me, even if she did have to fake it.

37

Facing Discouragement and Doubt:
A Trip Through the Wilderness

I know what it's like to face fear, discouragement, and doubt over areas of my life. I'm sure you can relate as well. You struggle and fight and work to get areas in order only to get laid off at work or to constantly fall short or flat. No matter how hard you try. First of all, I admire you for your endurance and persistence. Let me encourage you to remind yourself that these struggles, although they may carry on for long periods of time, are only to last for a season. If they last too long and you find yourself fighting discouragement and depression, then likely you need counseling or encouragement or definitely a new way to do things. One thing I also guarantee you is if all else fails, prayer will work. Spend time reading spiritual books and praying and seeking wisdom. Sometimes you can get more movement by stopping in your tracks and taking time to realign and center yourself. The picture becomes clearer as God gives insight and revelation and wisdom in how to proceed. This isn't easy, especially for us type A personalities. However, it is necessary and pays off.

I have seen the most successful people face these trips through the wilderness. A trip through the wilderness is often described as long, hard, hot, hilly, cold, and oppressive; you sense a loss in direction, purpose, and state of being.

> **h³** HOWARD'S HELPFUL HINT: *Centered people know that life is full of seasons, and they recognize each season for what it is. A season is a finite period in time that does not last forever.*

Always remember that this is only a season and how we respond to each adventure and season determines our success. I, myself, have admitted that I can't seem to go on at times. I wanted to quit and even said I quit. The truth is that I really just didn't want to go on. My body and flesh were tired and discouraged. It wasn't that I couldn't, it was that I didn't really want to take the pain and discomfort to pay the price. I hope you understand this and are reading it so we can understand we are all fallible and human. Everyone at sometime in life is faced with quitting or going on. Those of us who will reach success are those who choose to persevere and pay the price of success. I know this is hard at times when someone we love brings a season upon us through his or her carelessness or bad decisions. A company goes bankrupt and you are left jobless without retirement because of corporate theft or ignorance. Maybe you have a pregnant, unwed daughter at a young age, or a spouse who walked out on a marriage. Perhaps the newspaper reads of a child killed because of someone else's negligence. I know it is hard to think of it as a season. But the only way to proceed is to persevere through those times and move to the next, hopefully, happier season. I acknowledge it isn't easy, and I do not pretend to underestimate the pain you must be going through. It is just that, at some point, we all have to make the very tough decision to move on for our own mental health and to regain a certain level of stability and control. I have often heard loved ones state that when someone close to them dies, they don't get over it, they just get through it. Allow God to help you; don't push him away during this time.

Sometimes I find I respond well and other times I respond in a less than admirable way. Either way, I pay a price. I determine what price I pay and how severe. If I lash out at others and walk around discouraged and feeling sorry for myself, the season seems to last forever. If I choose to walk in love and faith and kindness no matter what my circumstances, I find it doesn't seem to last as long.

I'm in that wilderness even as I write this. I have taken steps to leave my current position and start a new path and job and career. It wasn't well planned out; however the timing seemed right. Time will tell. Remember I said I walk this talk. I will share later how it turned out. From my past experiences and reliance on God, everything will turn out fine. There may be pain and tears shed along the way. But the price I pay will be worth the reward.

38

WHY ALL THIS TALK ABOUT
SPIRITUAL CENTEREDNESS?

I'm sure by now you are wondering why I mention God so much or give him so much credit. I believe God loves us and has a plan for us. Read Jeremiah 29:11. Though verse 11 is good, it's when I see verse 13 that tells me it's when I seek him that I find him. I can't find him unless I do something. Such as seek for him. God gives us the strength to live move and have our being as seen in Deuteronomy 28. I truly believe we often give God much of the blame when he wasn't involved, and too much credit when he also wasn't involved. What, God isn't always involved? Precisely. How many people do you know that just make a decision to move to another place and never consult God and ask his will? Then, when they move and face problems and feel like a fish out of water the first person they blame is God. Let me let you in on a secret. God is only involved if you involve him! "Well if God hadn't let me leave I would never have gotten into this mess." The issue is often we do things without seeking the spiritual centeredness required and then we get angry and blame something other than ourselves. It couldn't possibly be our fault. I'm a victim of circumstance. No, you are a victim of your lack of seeking knowledge or God.

I have learned that God directs our footsteps when we involve him. The Proverbs bear this out. Read Proverbs 16. I have no problem giving God credit for my life because I rely on him so much and owe him so much for success. Psalms 37:23 (NLT) states, *"The Lord directs the steps of the Godly. He delights in every detail of their lives. Though they stumble they will never fall, for the Lord holds them by the hand."* He isn't a crutch or an excuse. He isn't religion, He is a chosen faith. After all I have been through, I will not deny him now. I have denied him in the past when I was weak and fearful. I pray that was the last time I ever deny him publicly. No job or career or amount of money or fear in any problem is worth denying God.

> **h³** HOWARD'S HELPFUL HINT: *Centered people develop a foundation of value in which to move and have their being.*

My foundation is spiritual. If my spiritual life is out of line as mentioned earlier, then everything else seems to get quickly out of whack. It's when I refocus and center upon God that all my work seems to flow effortlessly through my conscience. For some, their foundation is built upon something different. For others it may be money, family, or career. I never found that I could rely on those things for my total joy and reason for being. They are fallible, God isn't.

> **h³** HOWARD'S HELPFUL HINT: *Remember we are holistic beings. If one thing is out of balance, the whole thing doesn't work right. When you experience being out of balance, go to the area of concern and by dealing with it balance will be restored.*

39

CENTERED PEOPLE LEARN
TO SUFFER QUIETLY

How many books or lectures do you attend on suffering? Until recently, I have come across very few. No one likes to talk or think about suffering. In America, we think we shouldn't suffer or something is wrong. Something may be wrong. However, I believe the mindset that we shouldn't suffer is wrong. It is actually a privilege. I Peter 4:12–13 (TLB) states:

> Dear friends don't be bewildered or surprised when you go through fiery trials ahead, for this is no strange unusual thing that is going to happen to you. Instead be glad-because these trials will make you partners with Christ in his suffering and afterwards you will have the wonderful joy of sharing his glory in that coming day when it will be displayed.

We don't have to suffer; we get to suffer! What this scripture is saying is that we will experience suffering. So don't let it surprise you, but grow through it and reap your reward. I have friends who suffer physically in ways I will never suffer. However, because I have suffered in other areas I can relate to them. People who have suffered have a kindred spirit about them. I find what they bear physically isn't something I think I could bear, and what I suffer emotionally is something they say they couldn't handle. But you see, we both suffered. My good brother, Tim O'Brien, understands this concept with me. Tim showed me the verse in 2 Corinthians 1:4 that states, *"He [God] comforts us in all our troubles so that we can comfort others. When others are troubled we will be able to give them the same comfort God has given us."* We often act like it was God who brought the pain, when in fact it was God who brought the comfort for us during our pain. One year, the day after Christmas, the Lord impressed upon me to stop and see Tim. I had felt the leading to do this for several years when I would be visiting during the holidays, but I wasn't obedient to the Lord. I stopped by, and Tim and I had a great several hours of fellowship. We shared our suffering experiences and related to each other as Christian brothers should. Tim's family was in the living room, but we wanted to speak in private. So we went to Tim's bedroom. Tim has a king-size bed. He was lying on top of the covers, and I was lying on the other end.

I said, "Tim who would have ever planned this—you and I, the day after Christmas, lying in bed and sharing Christ?" This was humorous. We laughed and then I threatened him. I said, "Not a word of this to anyone. I have a reputation to protect." We had a blast sharing the Lord together that day.

Once, I had someone tell me thanks for being Tim's friend. I got a little angry about that comment. They didn't mean it in a bad way. They just knew Tim's physical condition required dialysis, which doesn't allow him much time for running with friends. However, I just gently corrected them and said "No, Tim is my friend!" Tim isn't a victim although he has been through the fire of life. There is a lot of depth in my friend. Tim has invested in me and given me comfort through prayer and listening to my pity parties. I am lucky to have such a good, honorable, godly friend.

So you may be wondering—how do I suffer like Christ suffered? Have you ever had a close loved one tell you they didn't love you anymore? Or a close friend decides to leave you and never speak to you again? Ever had someone betray your confidence and talk behind your back or plan you harm? Have you suffered in your body? So has Christ. So you see when you suffer as Christ suffered, you actually share in his sufferings and reap a reward for it. Have you ever had someone reject you because you were a Christian? God knows what you are experiencing and he doesn't leave you alone during those times, even if it feels like it. He is there upholding you with his righteous right hand. See Isaiah 41:10–13 (TLB),

> Fear not for I am with you. Be not dismayed for I am your God. I will strengthen you. I will uphold you with my righteous right hand. Behold all those who were incensed against you shall be ashamed and disgraced, they shall be as nothing, and those who strive against you shall perish. For I the Lord your God will hold your right hand saying to you, fear not I will help you.

God guarantees you he will help you when these things happen. He also deals with those who come against you. You don't have to. You choose to forgive and move on and place them in God's hands, and he will deal with them far better than you and I could have ever done. He may even lead them to repentance, which is great. I noticed when I decided to embrace those times of suffering I found myself much closer to Christ.

h³   HOWARD'S HELPFUL HINT: *Centered People learn to embrace times of suffering in a healthy manner.*

One thing I am still learning to do is to quietly learn to suffer. When I am suffering, I want everyone to know. How many people do you know who are like that? They think others ought to suffer with them and help bear their burden. It's all about me, me, and me! Now how unrealistic is that? In this life we are pretty much guaranteed failure and trials and tests that seem to balance the success and joys of life. I just don't allow the suffering to take my joy. My joy isn't based upon money or prestige or worldly possessions. If all those pass, I still have God and peace of mind. That's my joy. Even in suffering. No one wants to be around when we are cranky, self- centered, and moping. People want to be around happy, joyful, fun, easygoing people. We like going to movies and parades and ballgames, not funerals. People have enough problems of their own without having to carry ours. Sometimes we need to ask others for prayer. I certainly do. I want my seasons of suffering to be a short as possible. My last name is Lull. Look it up in the dictionary. It means "harmony." I love to live in a harmonic state of being. So the less I have to suffer, the better. [laughing] Let's all learn to suffer quietly.

40

Make an Effort to Help Those Who are Suffering

Everyday, I read the obituary columns to see if anyone I know has passed away. My heart grieves when I read of young couples losing a baby or parents losing a child prematurely. I stop and pray for them and ask God to send people their way to help share in the suffering and comfort them. We really don't know how blessed we are to have not had to experience those things. I have hugged grown, strong men who cried like babies when they lost a child, even when that child was in their 30's and 40's. Parents should never have to bear the burden of burying a child. And if it befalls on them, they shouldn't have to bear it alone. When I see someone suffering, I can't just walk by. I have to help, even if it's just to speak and acknowledge them. Give him a physical pat on the back or hug. That investment of time may have been just what he needed that day. To know someone cared for him. I can't honestly know everything they are experiencing but when my heart is open to the Lord and sensitive to people and their sufferings then I can share in it with them and possibly help in ways not thought of. How many times have I told someone, "I understand how you feel" only to have them respond with, "You can't possibly know I how I feel." Or they slap you up side the head. "You can't possibly know what I am going through?" Okay, I agree, but I don't feel the pressure to have to know. It doesn't make me less because I haven't felt as bad as they are feeling. I just realize they usually are so hurt they lash out in anger. Let's make a decision to shoulder that burden for them and forgive them and not take it personally. Continue to be there for them. Our shoulders are broad enough that we can bear that burden with them in their times of hurting. Face it, many of us like to know people care for us. I hope we haven't grown so cold that we walk right past the suffering and don't even acknowledge them. After being verbally slapped a few times, I have also learned to rephrase my "I understand how you feel" to "I understand you are hurting and I am here for you." See, even I can learn after getting slapped a few times.

If you see someone else suffering, whether it's professionally, financially, personally, medically, or whatever the cause, make a choice to help them out. People need to know we care.

> **h³** HOWARD'S HELPFUL HINT: *Centered people suffer quietly and help the suffering quietly.*

I don't need pats on the back. I need to help others who are God's gifts in the form of people when they need it most. Help them to return to being who they are as our brothers and sisters.

I often find that when I'm suffering and I make a conscious effort to help others, that it takes my eyes off myself, and by helping them, it actually eases my suffering. Funny how that works, isn't it? It's hard to feel sorry for myself when I'm focused on others.

41

CENTERED PEOPLE KNOW THAT
FORGIVENESS IS THE KEY TO FREEDOM

You are probably wondering how in the world one could over-come these obstacles and challenges and not be bitter. Earlier I stated we aren't victims.

> **h³** HOWARD'S HELPFUL HINT: *Centered People understand that even if they have been wronged or victimized, it doesn't mean they have to walk around with the spirit of being a victim.*

I have spoken to victims of violence you would never know have been violated. I have spoken to families that have been through untold atrocities. You couldn't tell it because they weren't walking in the spirit of being a victim and had learned to forgive. It was a process for them. I, too, have chosen to for-give. I choose a forgiving spirit to walk around in. When I did, I found that all that was binding me released. I reemphasize, this isn't easy, no way, no how. But centered people don't always take the easy road, do we?

42

MARATHONS AND THE LESSONS LEARNED

> **HOWARD'S HELPFUL HINT:** *Centered people do the hard things and do them right.*

I have run twelve marathons and many other races. I have always been an amateur athlete. I have never known a life of not exercising. When I was young, I loved to run like a deer. The feeling of weightlessness and speed was fun. Later in life, I ran to keep in shape not just compete. It was during the thirteenth marathon when a windstorm came, so they decided to call it half way through and it was only a half marathon. However, they gave us the medal because of all the training we had done. I learned a lot as I prepared for and ran races. No two runs were the same nor predictable. Either the weather affected us or hills or pace or training. My running joke (no pun intended) was the 5 H's. *Howard Hates Heat, Hills, and Humidity.* All those were killers to running a great race and made preparation crucial. While running, I learned the following and use these lessons in life today. Have the courage to get in the game. Be prepared to do your best and not win. It's okay. The following are comparisons to life and business I learned while preparing for and running marathons.

Preparation. This is where you win or lose a race. You run like you prepare and train. If I trained and prepared at a seven minute pace, then I ran the race at that pace. If I trained slower, I ran slower. Nothing beats preparation. Businesses understand that if they aren't prepared, then what they are truly doing is preparing to fail by losing consumer confidence in them and their product.

Pay the price. If I paid the price, I won. If I wasn't willing to, I didn't. In other words, if I did the necessary training to be successful then I succeeded. If I didn't, then I paid a price that was worse than if I had actually paid the right price in the first place. Most successful businesses understand by taking short cuts and not paying the full price for success as defined by their profession guarantees failure.

Focus on what each race requires. Nothing took the place of running. I couldn't cross train my way to success by biking more than running. I had to focus on what the race required. In life and business, there are many seasons. There are seasons of preparation and seasons of financing and seasons of building and seasons of maintaining and so on. Focus on what is necessary to make each season a success.

Prepare holistically your mind, body, and spirit. I had to prepare my mind and spirit as much as I did my body. I had to believe I could run farther than I ever ran before and I could do it faster each time. In life and business you are faced with many challenges that will catch you by surprise. You can minimize the impact of the surprise by preparing holistically and not leaving any area out. I read where a basketball team lost to a lesser talented team. The coach of the winning team stated that her team had come out with a higher level of intensity and caught the other team off guard, and they could never recover. Any good team should always prepare for the hardest thing they may face. Then, when it doesn't happen they can readjust and take over. It is a shame to a company or team to get caught off guard when they could have prepared for everything.

It takes commitment. I have to do the hard things in the right in order to succeed. By slacking I would certainly fail. Not paying attention to detail would guarantee failure. I find many businesses and people in life that just aren't prepared to make a full commitment. They are short-sighted and can't see the pitfalls of a lack of commitment. Good leadership should always prepare to make sure the commitment is there from anyone associated with his or her team and company. The same is true with your life. Always make sure those closest to you have the same commitment to your success as you do.

Passion and desire are necessary to maintain stamina and fulfill your dream. Have you ever seen a business that lacked passion and desire? Have you ever seen a person who is going through life without a passion or desire? You may not have. The reason is they won't be around for long. At least not in your circles. Let passion and desire stay stirred in your heart and spirit as you move into your calling and centered life.

Finishing is just as important as winning. The race winners were gifted world-class runners. The rest of us winners were winners because we finished the race. When we finished, we won our race. I never left a race unfinished. World-class runners, if they cramped or weren't going to win, may drop out of a race. I never dropped out after putting in all that preparation. I even collapsed with a muscle cramp at the end of a marathon in Colorado. However I did finish. Life will present to you the opportunity to drop out or quit. Remember, the reward goes to the finishers not just the winners. No matter what level of success a business or person may have had, I guarantee you that they had times of wanting to quit as well. That hits us all. Make the determined decision today you aren't going to quit and take a seat in the game of life to just be an onlooker.

Listen to your body. Leave out the ingredients for success and it may cost you your Life. I ran in one race where two died and one was taken by ambulance to the hospital. No race is worth that. Listen to the signs your body is sending you. In life and business, one has to listen for the same signs. Perhaps you weren't as prepared as you found you should have been. You may encounter things that you couldn't have foreseen until you were down the road a ways. It's okay as long as you have your eyes open and are willing to make the necessary adjustments.

The feeling of finishing a well-run race can't be replaced by anything else. Less than one percent of the total world population has run a marathon. Less than .002% have run more than two. I ran twelve; that places me in elite company. When you score big in life or business, you experience the euphoria that comes from having done a good job. You don't have to be in elite company to feel this and experience it. Every race is different and every sense of accomplishment is different. Share them with loved ones and coworkers and continue to move on to the next fun, successful adventure.

Rest is where you build your endurance. You don't build endurance by running your body down. You build it by training hard and allowing your body to rest and set a new higher level than before. I asked Olympic silver medalist Greta Waitz how she ran so fast. Her response to me was "How do you run for four hours? I couldn't possibly do that." Good perspective. We all can do things others can't. In life and business, you have to know when it is time to rest and when it is time to move forward. Getting the proper rest restores vision and fortitude and helps you to feel good about moving forward.

Enjoy the time you run and the people you run with. It doesn't last forever. Guys I have run with have died of health issues but left me memories I will never forget. I hold them dear to my heart. The medals mean little to me. They are signs that I did it. The medals bring back memories of the races and people I raced with, but they never replaced any of those people. I have spoken with many Olympic medalists and many world record holders. I was a sports enthusiast and autograph hound. They were all good people, who loved to run and paid the price. One thing I found fascinating was that after a year or so post-race, none of them remembered exactly where their medals were stored. Jim Ryun, Olympic silver medalist in Mexico City and one time world record holder in the mile said, "I think it's in a drawer upstairs in my house." Some had given the medals to their university or town hall for all to enjoy. After setting their goals of winning the medal, they found a humility that only those who have paid the price can experience. When they talk, they tell you they learned it wasn't the medal they cherished, it was the people and the experience. The same goes in business and life. The goal isn't the reward. The reward is found in the journey. Roger Bannister, the first person to ever run a sub 4-minute mile, stated his greatest accomplishment and joy was actually becoming a physician and enjoying his life's endeavors professionally.

Be a student of the sport. Study it. Study people. Eat, drink, and breath your passion. Let it become you. In life and business I have seen too many people who weren't a fit in different organizations. How many professional athletes have you seen leave their current team and go to a team they fit in with and win a championship? To be a fit, you have to allow the passion of the sport, business, and relationship to consume you to the point you love it and can't see yourself doing anything different at that point in your life.

In running marathons and life and business, you have to invest in yourself and others for success. The exhilaration is indescribable. I guarantee you it will be hard work mixed with rewards of success and failure. However, the price is worth paying. Remember, the highest quality items you can purchase are most expensive. They cost you the most. In life and business it is no different. If you want the best or desire to be the best, then pay the highest price.

The First Level 2 Trauma Center Designated

In the early 1990's, the state of Missouri had written new guidelines for how emergency rooms and trauma centers should run. They then asked all who wanted to be designated to apply and go thru the inspection process. I was hired as the new trauma nurse coordinator and had to learn quickly about things I knew absolutely nothing about. It was challenging and I worked tirelessly to influence others to help me make this happen. I inspired them to take ownership of the process. After all, it was about a system not a department or one person. I had people curse at me who didn't agree we should pay the price of being a center designated to quality trauma care. After all, they would say, the patients are going to come here anyway. I was like okay so we should just stay in mediocrity because we get them anyway? They thought we couldn't get any better than we were.

> **h3** HOWARD'S HELPFUL HINT: *Centered people know you can get better!*

I timed them in how long it took patients who came to the ER to when they went to x-ray. Could we shorten the golden hour? The golden hour was a phrase used to state that you had one hour to get someone from the scene of an accident into an operating room and tie off what is bleeding to save their life. After that hour, their odds for survival decreased. The results were astonishing and eventually in some case we cut up to thirty to sixty minutes off the delays to getting patients the care they needed. I could only do this because the people bought into the fact that we could get better, and I know they wanted to get better. They just needed a leader and a challenge. I learned just as much from them as they did from me.

When the inspection took place, the lead surgeon was condescending to me and was cad in his language. He took my system I had worked so hard on and tore it to pieces. Afterwards, he said to my CEO and others, "85 percent of what you do is good to excellent; now let's talk about the other 15 percent." I was devastated. I had never poured so much of myself into something only to be told I had failed. We were given six months to clean up the other 15 percent. My administrator said to me afterwards that he had been through many healthcare and state inspections but none as nasty as that one. I took some solace in that. My CEO, Lowell C. Kruse, said, "It's okay; you did a nice job, they don't come here to tell you how good you are." But I still felt like a failure. I wanted the success so badly I could taste it. I was so prepared I knew exactly where they would hit us. I knew all our weaknesses, but I also knew we didn't have time to totally overcome them before the inspection. So, we identified them and then showed where we had begun improvements. It just wasn't good enough for them. They wanted more time to produce more results.

> **h³**
>
> HOWARD'S HELPFUL HINT: *Centered people understand that life is like a trauma patient. At times it's not what I see that bothers me it is what I am not seeing that concerns me.*

With trauma patients, they may have an open laceration and bleeding, but they have a low blood pressure. Why is their pressure low? It is usually because they are bleeding internally. However, we can't see it. We see and measure the affects of it. We, as trained professionals, need to get them to the operating room and stop the bleeding and save their life. Life is like that; it is not always obvious to us that certain failure is around the corner, but unless we recognize it, it will hit us. Learn to look for what you don't immediately see.

How many marriages failed because a partner didn't protect their marriage? They often say I just didn't see it coming. I have heard some say business failure and bankruptcies are like that. The market changed, and I didn't see it coming. Well, now we understand life still comes at us whether we see it or not. Let's learn to look for it.

Back to the trauma center designation. Over the next six months, we worked to improve things and when the state came back to re-inspect us we passed and were the first Level 2 trauma center in Missouri designated under the new regulations. We were also only the second trauma center to be designated in the state. And we were the last inspected that year. That was quite an accomplishment. I still admire and owe many thanks to the people and physicians like ER Medical Chief of Staff, Michael Dunlap, and the Trauma Chief of Staff, Ed Andres, and Scott Koelliker, Director of the ED, Hopsital Administration for their commitment to the patients and staff and to all my nursing and paramedic and ancillary professionals who paid the price for success.

During the celebration and the department of EMS coming to give us our plaque and dedication, I stood back from the crowd and just watched the joy in their eyes and the sense of accomplishment as they attained and took pride in their work well done. That day, I knew what a coach felt like watching his players win a World Series or Super Bowl. We won ours. All the hard work, late nights, pain and pressure, offenses and insults taken and given had come to make us better healthcare providers and professionals who truly cared for the community. All I did was influence them and coach and teach them about regulations, and they in turn made me successful.

> h³
>
> HOWARD'S HELPFUL HINT: *Centered people know if they invest in others then the others will take care of the rest.*

Some won't help you no matter what, but they are the exception and can be filtered out of the organizations, culture, or relationship in a healthy manner. That was my coming of age as a healthcare professional. The pain of disappointment a year earlier was erased as I shared the joy and recognition that we really were good at what we poured ourselves into, as it was being recognized by others.

43

IT WASN'T MY FAULT, BUT...

I was speaking with a good friend of mine, Dr. David Thompson, who is an ER Physician and a board member in the Air Helicopter Rescue and EMS system in the USA. I was telling him of my decision to leave my current position and pursue career opportunities I had desired to do for some time. One of the things that I was reminded of was the people I consulted before making the move professionally and their advice. I had come to a place where I no longer felt like a fit within the organization I was in. The landscape had changed, and I had changed and I had accomplished the things I had desired to do and wanted to leave while my successes were still evident to all. I struggled to make sense of the timing and the purpose for the move and why I didn't feel like a fit. All I knew was that it was time to make such a move. Instead of taxing myself with the why questions, I just had to realize that it wasn't my fault, but it happened anyway. I still had to deal with it. I encourage you to read John G. Miller's book *QBQ: The Question Behind the Question*. John tells how to avoid asking the "Why me?" questions.

> **HOWARD'S HELPFUL HINT:** *Centered people always look at themselves first to see if there is or was anything they can do or could have done differently to change the situation or how they feel.*
>
> h³

This is because they aren't blaming others and they know they are ultimately responsible for their outcomes. When I spoke with a colleague of mine in Houston, she very professionally but curtly said, "Howard, look; you can't place blame on you or the institution. Every day people find they have outgrown or no longer are a fit with an organization, and they just move on. It's not you so quit trying to fix it. Just move on." I was a little taken aback but also felt how refreshing it was to actually have a colleague be so forthright with me. She stated it in a matter of "I said it and that settles it" sort of way. I find that colleagues like that give me the time of day because they like me. They aren't being rude. I love a frank reply when it is done appropriately.

I was always so used to seeing people fired or leave organizations because of a failure, not because of successes. So I had wrongly figured that I must have failed in some sort of way to feel like this. The truth was that it wasn't my fault, but I still had ownership and needed to move on and not make it like a slow amputation. I spoke with my boss, and together we made a decision to have my departure occur in a healthy manner. I wouldn't have it any other way. I will always leave an organization better than I found it if it depends upon my actions alone.

You may feel the same way or be going through something similar in your life. We type A personalities always feel like we have to have the answers before we can make the move with certainty. I have found that oftentimes when you walk in faith, you make the move and then the answers seem to fall into place. This isn't blind faith. It isn't presumption. It is a knowing. It does have some planning and calculation to it. Placing blame or having it figured out before you make the decision to move doesn't have to happen. Just the fact you know in the end that with God it will be okay. You can still move forward. You see, your attitude of moving forward isn't one of rebellion. It is one of a healthy fear of the Lord and respect for your career, knowing possible consequences. Oftentimes it is after you have removed yourself from a situation that you see it so much more clearly than when you were in the middle of it. It's hard to see in the middle of a storm. Once the storm blows over, you can see what happened. Give yourself space and time and during the reflective seasons you go through it will become clearer.

> **HOWARD'S HELPFUL HINT:** *Centered people realize that by removing themselves from a situation they gain better perspective and insight.*

44

CENTERED PEOPLE LEAVE A LEGACY

I was watching an interview by Tim Russert. He was interviewing Susan St. James, whose fourteen-year-old son died in a plane crash on his way to private school. Another son, who was also in the crash, pulled her husband, NBC sports director Dick Eborsold, from the crash. I admired Susan as she bravely appeared and spoke so lovingly and eloquently of her son and family. After the crash, the school gave her Teddy's papers. In them was an autobiography that Teddy had written. The school required, at the end of eighth grade, that their students write one. He stated, "Crossing the finish line is just the beginning of the greatest journey." He spoke of his love for God and his family. How wise Teddy was and what great introspective insight he had carried with him and expressed so lovingly to his family. What a great gift Susan and Dick must feel they possess with that insight Teddy shared. I hope I have that written correctly. The interviewer asked her about her faith and Susan stated, "People say God causes this or that; I don't believe it. We live in a free world with free wills." She then stated something very profound. "To hold resentment is like drinking poison and hoping the other person dies." In other words, resentment only poisons the one carrying it and holding on to it. Forgive, and get on with life. Cherish what good times you had. Don't carry baggage that isn't worth carrying or distracts you from the joys of life. Oh yes, Susan was obviously grieving and missing her son terribly, but she was focusing on the great fourteen years she had just spent with a wonderful son. She went on to say, "Teddy is in heaven now, holding our seats for us until we arrive." You may want to see the December 3, 2004 Today Show interview with Tim Russert for the exact quotes. I have paraphrased the best I remembered. I was so moved to see her act so bravely. All this brings me to my next point.

> **h³** HOWARD'S HELPFUL HINT: *Centered people desire and work towards leaving a legacy.*

They leave something others can benefit from for generations to come. Look at all the men and women mentioned in scripture. Look at the presidents, statesmen, pastors, and evangelist of the past. Read their books. You will find humble, strong men and strong women full of passion and desire

What legacy do you want to leave? I ask some people that and they give me the "you're nuts" look. They give me that "I just want to pay the bills sort of look." I'm used to that look now so it doesn't bother me any more when I get it. Teddy Ebersold at fourteen years of age left a legacy of love and wisdom. Think of the wisdom he had to write what he did in his autobiography. I know people today who will never leave a legacy, nor will they write even their own obituary column. Be known for doing something and contributing more than just earning a paycheck. I am not underestimating the hard times families have to raise families and work jobs and pay taxes, bury loved ones and live life. But amidst all that, find the legacy that is deep within your heart that you so desire to give and leave our society with. At the very least, leave your family with one. I think a creative job someone should do is interview families who want to leave legacies and place them on DVDs for families to remember loved ones and perhaps even play them at the funeral. That may sound a bit of a stretch for some of us, to think it isn't morbid or something. But what better way to remember them and honor them one last time with family and friends gathered? I have been called and asked to speak about friends of mine who passed on, and I take my time to remember what it was about them that I truly admired and was blessed by in the relationship I had with them. The legacy I speak of is the investment they made in me in their short time on the earth. The love and friendship they shared with me. Get past the feeling that you aren't worth anything, that all you are is a boring eight to five daily worker. No, you are so much more. You are fathers, mothers, sons, daughters, neighbors, employees, employers, scientist, postal workers, doctors, teachers, nurses, soldiers, day-care workers; the list goes on and on.

My dad was a career soldier who served in Vietnam. He lost his life there. His name is proudly displayed on the Vietnam memorial. To this day, I tell people I know going to Washington D.C. to go by the wall look his name up and tell my dad thank you. I can't go by the wall even in my 40's without crying. His legacy is that he cared for people and gave his life for others so that they may experience the freedoms he so much believed in. That wall is filled with many names of men and women who left the same legacy. That is so honorable. That is the ultimate legacy of giving your life for another. The Bible says God did that too. Read John 3:16. No matter what we do or have done, we have someone who has gone before us.

I am saying you are people who love and are loved. The ones I just listed have served society and leave a legacy of service to the lives they touch. They lived for things bigger than themselves. Teddy and I never met, but look how I was blessed learning of his life and his contribution. You don't have to have done something that made national headlines to leave a legacy. You just have to be cognizant that you are leaving a legacy, whether you know it or not and that you need to choose what the legacy is. I am so thankful that mothers are leaving legacies of children, well-loved, disciplined, and cared for, who now serve our society. We see the investment these mothers have made as we see our presidents, congressmen, and women and others. We don't see their moms but we see the legacy their loving moms gave us. Having been a loving and caring mother and father is the greatest legacy anyone can leave. That's because we are molding, shaping, and investing in another person's life.

I don't want to sound depressing; however, as I write this, children are being born, people are dying, people are graduating college, people are starting college, people are getting married, people are splitting marriages, and people are making decisions that affect millions or even just two or three. The world is in constant motion. We live in a complex world, and I thank God daily I'm not God. What a job he has. God sits on the throne of heaven with his son at his right hand and he isn't shaken or caught off guard by any of it. The world keeps going even though all those things are happening. We all have a sphere of influence we walk in daily. Allow me to challenge you to leave a legacy and to write your legacy in your own words.

45

My Legacy: He Cared

I want my final legacy to be that "He Cared." That's what I want written on my stone when I'm laid to rest. That's what I want people to know and remember of me, simply that I cared. I cared enough to pray with you, cry with you, and share joyous events such as your children's successes, graduations and marriages, the births of your grandchildren, your promotions, and I loved to share life itself. Through the good and bad, I was there caring for you and caring what happened to you. I hope you can write volumes of what I did, but what is written is just the proof that I cared. I have a sports collection of football helmets, autographs, baseballs, bats, etc. that I have displayed in my home. I love the nostalgic. I have autographs of people who are far from being famous because I had them sign something for me to help me remember the great experience I had of knowing them. They serve as reminders to me of the people I met and no longer are with us. They remind me of the beautiful days I sat at a place like West Point and watched football in historic Miche Stadium. The time I shared the Army/Navy game with my son on a trip to Philadelphia after 911 and how we all felt as one in that stadium together as the president came out to greet us.

I love eating lunches with my daughter. I love to eat, and sharing a meal with her is always fun. I love the great experiences of life with my wife—the many Christmases with family, the time I went to Cambridge, Massachusetts, and watched Harvard beat Yale 35–3 and met Neal, and Amy Bernie and others you will never know. You see, it's not the collection I'm proud of or carry in my heart, but if, God forbid, the house burned and they were gone, I still have the legacy of all I experienced in my heart. That's the message I'm trying to relay to you. I cared, and I cared about the right things in life. I cared about people, and I cared about life. When I go places and a friend of mine comes to mind, I send them a t-shirt and let them know that even though they weren't with me in person, they were in my heart. See, mom, you did do okay. That's my legacy. I hope the people I met along the way and shared life with would agree with me.

> **h³** HOWARD'S HELPFUL HINT: *Centered people understand that life is a gift; they don't take it for granted.*

As a registered nurse in the emergency room, I experienced things that absolutely broke my heart. These experiences gave me an appreciation for life and helped center me to what is important. They were experiences I was called to walk in but wouldn't if I didn't have to. I worked with a good friend. She had a beautiful little baby girl with strawberry blonde hair. She would dress her daughter in the cutest little dresses and bring her for us to hold. One day, over the EMS radio we heard a call go out to an address we all recognized. It was hers. Then the worst news we could have imagined was called to us. The paramedics called to say they were attempting to resuscitate a baby with possible SIDS. It was that precious angel that gave us so much joy. We did everything we could to resuscitate her, but to no avail. She went to be with the other precious angels God holds so close to his heart until we are reunited with them. I was a new nurse and grieved that I hadn't done enough. I also had to prepare the baby for her family to come in and grieve and see her before we sent her to the funeral home. I will never forget seeing a family that had their hearts torn and ripped from them—to see the look of devastation in my friend's eyes. I have never so carefully given care to a precious baby as I did then. She was their angel. She was our angel as she shared her brief life with us. It was a privilege for me to be able to care for her and her family.

Somehow, I believe God has these little angels waiting to be reunited with us when our time comes as well. I have had other close friends who have lost their dreams and babies prematurely. Once I asked the Lord that since his Word says He will never leave us nor forsake us, then how do these things happen? The Lord told me it is true he will never leave us nor forsake us, but our bodies do, sometimes our friends do, sometimes this world does. But God doesn't. This explanation isn't God's "get off free card." He doesn't need one. God doesn't get off easy seeing us suffer. He didn't get off easy seeing his son die and listening as his own son asked him why he forsook him. I personally believe God even grieved at that time. I haven't seen that written anywhere, but if God is a better father than any of us could be he surely must have grieved at watching his son's suffering. God isn't the blame; he is our answer.

My profession has caused me to be involved with people who are dying and comfort them until their deaths. There was an electrocution of a young man who looked me in the eyes and asked if he was going to die. I looked at him and said we are going to help you and take good care of you. He died seven days later. There was a five-year-old girl from a car accident who looked up at me and asked me if her mommy had died. Her mommy was laying in the next room over, having been killed in the accident. I said we are trying to help your mommy too. She said God had told her that her mommy was dead. I marveled at the courage this brave five-year-old had and the grace God had given her to handle the situation.

I had a call to come to the ED to help on a night before Thanksgiving. A drunk driver had broadsided the car of a wife who went to pick up her husband from work and had a toddler in the car seat. The mom ended up being okay, the dad died, and the baby had cuts and scrapes. The man who ran the light looked at me as he told a family member they couldn't get him on the same charge of drunk driving twice. He was claiming double jeopardy. I looked at him in anger and said to myself I would try to put him away when given the chance. He did have to go to jail again. He lost. His arrogance cost him as it had cost others.

I developed a public anti-drinking campaign that nearly cost me my job. I had the ED team stand around an ED bed and hold an instrument we have to use on trauma victims. The caption read, "Go ahead and drink and drive, we will clean up afterward." It also listed that more than 8000 would lose their lives to drunk drivers. I ran it a year to the date of Thanksgiving eve in the newspaper. The public response was mixed but mostly angry with me for being so bold. I expected that. I did get some that wrote in and told people to get off my back. The end result—that Thanksgiving weekend the ad ran we didn't have any drinking and driving accidents. Coincidence? Nope, it was calculated. I offer no apologies for saving lives.

On Christmas, my colleagues were faced with tragedy as well. A man kidnapped his kids and shot and killed them in the presence of the police. The police shot him and wouldn't let EMS near him until they were sure all was clear. My colleagues had to try and resuscitate the child on Christmas and call the mom and tell her the news. Try that on for size. I have had to make these types of calls and they are hard to make and people don't like you when you call them with this news.

I hope I have given you a new appreciation for all our ER nurses and doctors and technicians. I salute them. I honor them as my brothers and sisters and colleagues for their dedication and courage. They are people just like you and me who have dreams, problems, and concerns and go through the trials of this life, yet choose to lay their lives down and help those who are ill and in need of help. Why write about this? Is it cleansing? Absolutely not! I embrace the impact these events have made in my life. I will always have to live with these memories. I want people to understand the life we have is so precious and time is so little that tomorrow and today won't look the same. It affects everyone. Give all you have to give. Live with little regret. *Regret is baggage best left lost at the airport of life.* Pray for society and your loved ones. Live life, and love life and cherish it as the true gift it is.

CENTERED PEOPLE KNOW GOD MEETS YOU RIGHT WHERE YOU ARE

I find it unique that the times we live in can be classified the "best of times, the worst of times." This year I have had the best time and most productive time ever spent in prayer and knowing God and his Word. However, every and I mean every area of my life has been attacked. That's correct, every area I have listed and written about in this book has been attacked and challenged. I have found that through these trials I haven't always responded the way I would think a man of God or Christian would respond. I was shocked by what I heard come out of my mouth towards God and others. I have learned that God wasn't shocked by my responses. He knew how I would respond long before I ever did. That's why I believe he has allowed certain trials in my life to help expose and reveal my true human character and the changes I would need to make. I can't make these changes on my own. I couldn't even recognize I needed the changes so how could I possibly know how to change. God allowed them to be revealed to me because he knows that with the calling he has on my life I would never make it by staying in the same condition I was in. All I know it was revealed I need more of Christ and the fruit of the spirit in my life. Without more of these characteristics of God in my life, how could I ever think I could move to a higher plane of living in him and moving in him and having my being in him? Remember it is by faith we live. I can't see tomorrow but God can. He knows. He loves me enough that he knows I need the change and the benefit the changes will bring in me and for others and me. God meets us right where we are. We don't have to clean up for him or put on our Sunday best. We just have to be real.

47

WE ARE THE CONSTRUCTION PROJECT,
GOD IS THE DESIGNER

You have heard the scripture, "He is the Potter we are the clay." There is so much truth in that small scripture. It truly shows the heart of the one admitting it. It is like one of us saying I want to make something of purpose out of the pile of steel I have. I want it to last. My project will have a lasting impact on others. It must have unusually good strength. So I need the best of my steel to make this. I look at all the steel I have, and I choose the steel I will use. I then mold it, shape it, design it. I apply the right amount of heat to it. You see, the steel won't bend unless I apply heat to it. The characteristic of steel is that it was made by fire so only fire can design it. You and I are the same way. Christ looks at all the Christians and says I need to use someone for a special project I have. In 2 Chronicles 16:9 (TLB) scripture states, *"For the eyes of the Lord search back and forth across the whole earth, looking for people whose hearts are perfect towards him, so that he can show his great power in helping them."* That doesn't mean you have to be sinless or a perfect person. Nor does it imply you are a passive participant that just allows fate to determine your course. It's a matter of the heart. It means that Christ is looking for a people whose heart is dedicated to him—that no matter what the call on you he may bring, no matter the design he has for you, that you are dedicated to him in ways that when he molds and shapes you, you will allow it to happen. You relieve yourself of being angry or insensitive to others. You do this even when you want to accuse God of seemingly not being fair with you, however knowing that in the end you didn't quit. You won't quit. You have come too far to quit, and no matter how painful, you will pay the price to have Christ, the creator of the universe, to work with you and use you mightily. When we realize we are made in the image of Christ, then we realize that the only thing that can shape us is Christ. Other things can have an affect on us, but only Christ can make sure, through his fire, that we get molded, shaped, designed, and built to Christ's expectations. It is often painful and we experience anger and runs of emotions and mis- understandings. Others close to us think we are weird and have lost our minds, but you still didn't quit. You know the price is well worth the pain. I have seen people shaped by bitterness who won't allow Christ to heal their hurts. My, how I hurt for them! I try to guard myself from becoming the same.

On a similar but lesser note, it is like watching those people who enter a contest to win a free car. The only catch is they have to keep one hand on the car longer than anyone else can. If they move their hand away, they lose. I have yet to hear a person who won one of the cars say it wasn't worth the price of discomfort they had to pay and go through to reach their victory—a much simpler example but you get the point. You pay the price and win. Remember, only you can do what Christ has for you. He not only called others, He called you. He is preparing you. Learn to walk in it. Relax in it as much as you can. Just like construction workers and designers, God is into seasonal repairs. He gives you time to center and enjoy the life he is unfolding for you.

> h³ HOWARD'S HELPFUL HINT: *Centered people learn to embrace the seasons of change.*

Seasons of change are uncomfortable. We move out of comfort zones, we go through growing pains; we hurt at times when we did nothing to cause the pain. Please don't think I am being insensitive to pains you have endured. I'm not. I have had deep pains as well. I just want you to know when I allowed God to take them and deal with them I became centered and well again. You may think you are past the point of attaining this. You aren't. God is upholding you with his righteous right hand and keeping you safe until his return. Embrace him and receive his embrace. I am better at saying this publicly or to you in private than I am in writing it. If I were there with you, I would be showing you God's compassion. Please receive this.

As an example, I find the teams in professional sports go through seasons of change. You ask, even the champions make changes? My response is yes, *especially* the champions. They have grown to realize that to be successful they have to make hard, gut-wrenching, eye-tearing, and crying decisions that affect others' lives. They make decisions that affect people they have spent hard times with, have grown with, and watched their families grow and be blessed and now in order for the organization to move forward or in another direction that person no longer fits in the plans. These are very hard lessons that most people avoid. Coaches and managers make cuts and hirings for reasons bigger than themselves or the individuals involved. In order for the whole organization to be successful changes must be made. Even changes that are extremely painful. I see people say it wasn't personal. But I disagree. If it involves a human being, we need to realize it is personal. At the very least to the person being changed it is. To experience a rejection hurts people, especially if they have poured their life and efforts into something, whether it's a marriage or job or relationship or team. Don't tell them it wasn't personal. Don't tell them the pain isn't real. I hate the fact that I see people treated in such a manner. I have been treated that way myself. To be rejected or told I no longer fit in was painful. I always asked myself what I did to cause these things to happen. I realized it wasn't necessarily me. It was a combination of things. I have learned to no longer let things affect me so much emotionally or personally. I do it by making a conscious decision that life is too short to worry about it. Just go on. I have found that God is so faithful that I will land on my feet somewhere and love it.

So it is with life. Are you willing to pay the price necessary to win the life Christ has for you? At times I question whether I want to go through the next phase God has for me. After all, I have a will. I can say no. I can tell Christ no. Or can I? Can I really say no to Christ and think I will live the life that only I choose? No, I can't. I may say no for a moment until I muster up the courage to go on. But I still find I go on. I laugh because I give myself the credit of going on. But to even make the decision to go on, I needed Christ's help. Let me further illustrate this lesson.

I was a new, green, fresh registered nurse going to work in an ER. I had all the proper training and certifications. My first week on the job, I was working when a code blue was coming in by ambulance. In other words this person had a heart attack and needed the best care we could provide. I was walking over to help out a little when one of the nurses in front of everybody there asked if I had ever been in charge of a code. I said, "No."

He said, "Well, now you are!"

My response was one of shock and I asked, "And you want this guy to live?" My role went from being an assistant to being in charge and responsible and accountable for this person's direct care. So I told the team assembled instructions to do and placed order to the chaos. The lesson I learned—and you need to get this too—was that the nurse giving me the assignment and my team were not going to let me fail. Oh yes, I thought it was all on me, but it wasn't. They carried the load too. They wanted to see me succeed. They wanted the patient to live and get great care. They knew the outcomes from all their experiences and knew I would be okay. Oh yes, I could have still blown it making bad decisions or not paying attention or even walking in fear. But they weren't going to let that happen. They weren't going to let my shortcomings determine the end result for that patient. Yes, the patient lived and so did I. Just as my colleagues weren't going to allow me to fail, God isn't going to allow us to completely fail either.

48

GOD KNOWS YOU AND HE ISN'T GOING
TO LET YOU COMPLETELY FAIL

What do I mean by this? We will experience failures. Centered people understand that failure is but a moment in time. But when you walk with God, he won't let the failures define you or disqualify you. Remember Peter denying Christ three times. This is the same Peter to whom Christ referred in Matthew 16:18 (NLT), "...and upon this rock I will build my church and the powers of hell will not conquer it," the same Peter who was devastated at his failures and decided to just go back fishing after Christ's death, the same Peter who took his eyes off Christ when walking on water and fell in the lake. My personal opinion is at least Peter got out of the boat and was willing to fail. You see, that's all Peter knew, Christ and fishing. So when one seemingly left and he failed, he returned to what he knew. When Mary and Salome and Mary Magdalene went to the tomb to place embalming spices on Jesus, they found the stone rolled away and an angel who was recorded in Mark 16:7 (TLB) stated, "Now go and give this message to his disciples including Peter." He mentioned Peter separately. I think Peter was so devastated at his own personal failure that he felt useless and like God would never have favor on him again. It must be hard in life to think that even God doesn't like you. But you see God isn't like that. You see, the job wasn't finished. Christ loved Peter so much, and he would never be finished loving Peter no matter how badly he failed. He is like that with us too. Christ didn't let Peter's failures or shortcomings define him or disqualify him from use in God's kingdom purposes. God used those failures to refine Peter for better use. After that, scripture recorded people would be healed just by passing under Peter's shadow. We must be careful in the church today to not so easily disqualify each other because of our failures.

> **h³** HOWARD'S HELPFUL HINT: *Centered people know that failure is but a tool in the hand of Christ to spur us on to greater accomplishments.*

God uses our seemed failures to spur us on to much greater accomplishments than we could imagine. In the book of Isaiah 55:8–9 (NLT), it states, *"My thoughts are nothing like your thoughts,' says the Lord. 'And my ways are higher than your ways and my thoughts are higher than your thoughts.'"* God's way of doing things isn't like man's ways of doing things. When we think we are doing what Jesus would do, we need to question if it's really what he would be doing. I think we need to seek his wisdom before making such a bold statement. Are we really doing what Jesus would do? Or are we doing what we think Jesus would do? I'm not talking about premarital sex and drugs; I'm talking about life and life's decisions. How many moves have we actually made without consulting the Lord and his wisdom? Kind of scary to think we have done so much under our own strength and leading isn't it?

Too many times, we allow men and women to determine our success or worthiness. What a huge mistake. Never

ever give someone that power in your life. Never place your self-esteem in someone else's hands. Give it all to God and succeed. God knows what to do with our failures. Several times I took my guilt and failures to Christ and saw him laughing and doing what he needed to do for me.

I almost hate writing this, but I have walked it and I do know something about it. By writing this, I hope you understand that I do understand what it is like to fail and be redeemed by God. Even to have the guilt cleansed is a huge relief. I have shed many tears and walked alone through the wilderness under God's protection. Christ will see you and me to the other side, *just as his father did him.*

Centered people get rid of all that is wrong.

There is a scripture, James 1:21 (TLB), that reads, *"So get rid of all that is wrong in your life both inside and outside and humbly be glad for the wonderful message we have received, for it is able to save our souls as it takes hold of our hearts."*

There is a twofold message I want to point out. The Lord showed me this scripture as I was struggling to live a life more free from carnal desires. Oh yes, I loved the Lord and had a good prayer life and saw most of my prayers answered. But God wanted and expected more from me.

> **h³**   HOWARD'S HELPFUL HINT: *Centered people are active in getting rid of all that hinders them from freedom in Christ.*

Sin is bondage. Anger is bondage. Selfishness is bondage. Anything that keeps you from experiencing and daily enjoying a vibrant, active relationship with God is bondage. What nation of people did you ever hear say they loved being in bondage? The intelligent nations cry out for a release from bondage. Armies storm other countries and capitals to release a nation of people in bondage. Bondage is a prison. Just ask an alcoholic or drug addict or sex addict. They oftentimes do what they hate because their will has been given over to the bondage of the substance, keeping them from being and doing what they truly desire deep in their souls. The word says that God came so we may have life and have it more abundantly. You can't have an abundant life living in bondage to sin and carnal desires. *Bondage makes you perform the will of another person or thing, while all the time trying to break you of your own free will.*

Read 2 Peter 2:19 (TLB), "...*For a man is a slave to whatever controls him.*" We all have had to deal with things that seem more powerful than we are. Stop allowing those things of bondage to control you. Nothing good ever came from being controlled by something to which you are enslaved. Determine now that you aren't going let anything other than your passion to serve God control and inspire you.

What James 1:21 is saying is that it is our responsibility to get rid of the things that aren't pleasing to God, both hidden and public. It is my responsibility to get rid of unhealthy channels I may watch in the privacy of my home when no one else can see me or know what I am doing. I can hide that. Truthfully, I can't hide it from God. So I am only fooling myself if I do such things.

Along those same lines, if I keep lust hidden in my heart for material things or anger in my heart that has caused me to not forgive someone for wronging me, then it is my responsibility to get rid of it. I can't just pray, "Oh God, take it from me." I need to pray, "Oh God, I give it to you. It was my sin I was carrying and I no longer desire to carry the baggage so I now actively give it to you."

I have men point at a beautiful woman and say to me, "Hey, look at that eye candy. She is gorgeous." I respond by looking and acknowledging she is. When I comment about them staring they usually say to me, "It doesn't hurt to look."

I say, "Oh really." How much I desire for people to know the Word of God. I say, "You know in the gospels there is a story of Jesus being in the wilderness and Satan coming to tempt him. In Matthew 4:8–9 (TLB) it states, "Then *Satan took Jesus to the peak of a very high mountain and Showed him the nations of the world and all their glory. I'll give it all to you he said, if you will only kneel and worship me.*" Even Satan knows the eyes to your soul are through the eyes of your head. You see, you can't desire what you can't see or imagine.

James 1:14 (TLB) states, "*Temptation is the pull of man's own evil thoughts and wishes. These evil thoughts lead to evil actions and afterwards the death penalty from God. So don't be misled my brethren.*" How many of us didn't care what our brides looked like and just placed ads in the paper for a smart women and then married them because of their IQ's? None of us did that. I know it sounds absurd. And don't send me a bunch of mean letters or emails. There are a lot of highly intelligent, beautiful women in this world. My daughter is one of them. My point is looking does have an affect. It can be good or bad, but either way it has an affect. Television commercials prove this. There have been times I have prayed that God deliver me from any unknown consequences I may have brought upon myself in being so ignorant of what his Word and desire is for my life. Look, we all have areas of compromise to overcome. That is why the Lord says we need him. If the designer of the human race says we need him, I think we would be wise to listen and obey him.

If you buy a car designed by the manufacturer and he says you have to put diesel fuel in this car then what do we think is going to happen if we put gasoline in that car? It probably won't work as the original designer and manufacturer intended. Or it may not work at all. That's why the second half of James 1:21 in TLB is so important. *"...for it is able to save our souls as it takes hold of our hearts."* There was a time in my life when I would sin in an area. I would always find myself running back to that particular sin. One day I was asking myself, "Why do I act like an eighteen-year-old and sin in that area? Do I have a cursing problem?" The Lord in his graciousness and mercy showed me that the cursing was just an outward manifestation of an inward anger problem. I didn't have a cursing problem or a porn problem or an alcohol problem; I had an anger problem. I just ran to cursing like an old friend. You know, an old friend who stabs you in the back and reminds you of failure, not really a good friend. I decided to pray scriptures daily, oftentimes repeating them and fighting spiritual warfare. I made the Word take hold of my heart. To this day, I write them on three by five cards and carry them in my pocket and pray them and memorize them, allowing the Word to take hold of my heart.

As the Word takes hold of your heart, you have no choice but to live what it says. You can't live any other way because the word now has taken over an area of your heart that was once occupied by sin, lust, anger, sickness, poverty, cheating, or whatever the word you received changed in you. When you go to sin, the Word you have been meditating on and memorizing and praying is now in the place of that sin. When you are tempted, the Holy Spirit reminds you of the word you have learning and it does a preemptive strike on that temptation so it doesn't manifest into a sin. As I mentioned earlier, you can't passively have the Word of God take hold of your heart. You have to actively, by faith, open your Bible and fellowship with the living, active, spoken Word of God. The Bible isn't a fairytale. It is more than a history book. It is like medicine. It has active ingredients. It is the actual spoken word of the actual creator of everything addressed to you and me, so we may be saved in all areas of our lives and be granted more in life than salvation of the soul. The Word is for the salvation of every area of your life. It is the antibiotic for any sickness in nature you may have.

Christ-centered people know this, and they don't miss the Word anymore than they miss breathing air. It is that crucial for them. It is their lifeline. They can't live without it. It has become their actual life source. Nothing else satisfies or gives them the life they desire except for the Word.

I see a whole generation of people who were raised in churches and Christian homes but actually only know God in their heads and not their hearts. To know God in your heart is to actively participate in a relationship with him. These people know God can bless, can heal, and can deliver. They have heard their parents' testimonies, yet they have never experienced God doing any of those things for them or have experienced it on a limited basis still leaving doubt if it was Christ or not. I'm not knocking being raised in a Christian home and church. Thank the Lord your parents had the wisdom to provide that for you. Now you have to act. No more childlikeness. Now it's growing up time. *We have to get past the point of the Bible being just a book to study and to relieve our conscience after we have done something we feel bad about. It is his spoken word of life to us, that we may find life and have it more abundantly.*

You do this by allowing the Word of God to take hold of your heart, just as James 1:21 says. Take the time to allow the Word of God to be planted in your heart and take deep roots. You are in eternity so get busy.

When you plant a garden, you don't just throw the seeds in the ground and then say, "Well, good luck. I hope you come up so I can eat you." No, what you do is your prepare the soil, you prepare it and soften it up. You add fertilizer to help the growth. You put up necessary barriers to keep the animals and bugs from coming in and stealing your seed. Once it's grown, you still have to protect it. Deer and other four-legged animals, things seen and unseen then desire it and will do almost anything to sneak in and steal it from you. Have you ever noticed that when someone or something is trying to steal from you they never do it during the daylight hours or when you can see them doing it? Sometimes they do but not often. You have to have a constant guard over your heart, protecting what's yours. Don't let the thief steal the Word from your life. Don't passively give your joy or body to another for his pleasure. You guard it with all your might. I, like others, have been guilty of not protecting areas of my life as well as I should have. Taking it for granted, I realized this after none too late. Centered people guard all areas of their lives.

I have seen boys date other men's daughters and take advantage of the daughter because they knew they could get away with it—not mine. When a boy came to my home, which was rare after word of my fatherly reputation got out, I let him know by the look in my eyes that under no circumstance should I ever catch wind of the thief trying to steal what is mine. He knew without a word being said that he would pay a price if mine came back in worse shape than when she left. Fact of the matter is that I would have as well. It wasn't a joke. I meant business. Christian or not, I would lay down my law. I even verbally spoke to young men letting them know there would be consequences. One smiled, and I said, "You think it's funny or that I'm joking?" He said, "No, Sir." I replied, "You really want to know what's funny? I am the one you read about who actually will do it." Then I laughed in his face. Needless to say, I didn't have any problems. I also taught my son how to treat a lady and guard her from the thief and taught him to not be a thief. I am proud of the gentleman he has become.

Men and women beware and alert for the scripture states in John 10:10 (NLT), *"The thief's purpose is to steal, kill, and destroy. My purpose is to give them a rich and satisfying life."* God showed me he came to heal, fill, and deploy. That's correct, He came to heal you of your past life by accepting him into your life. He came to fill you with the Holy Spirit for more power, and He came deploying you to the world so you may be his representation to all who meet you.

As I finish this thought, I leave you with this. How you feel and what you desire influence everything in your life. People will argue this with me, but I really don't care. I find that we work hard towards whatever we affectionately enjoy or desire. Those things I refer to as affections influence how we live, act, spend our money, and talk to our neighbors. In Proverbs 4:23 (TLB) it is written, *"Above all else guard your affections [heart] for they influence everything else in your life."* You have to guard your heart and keep out anything that would steal your affection for Christ and his will for your life. I assure you from my experiences this will keep you from much heartache and is worth all the effort you put into guarding and watching over it.

49

CENTERED PEOPLE KNOW THEY WERE BORN FOR A TIME LIKE THIS

To what time am I referring? I am referring to your time. The time in life when everything you have worked hard to become and serve and have dreamed about has now culminated in a specific time for you to perform where and when no one else could possibly do it. No one could replace your time or your calling. Only you can deliver the message or song or love like you were intended to do.

> **h³** HOWARD'S HELPFUL HINT: *Centered people are aware of the season of calling they are currently in.*

Don't allow your season to pass by. We have all witnessed generation after generation being born and dying off without contributing. Make sure you have prepared enough to contribute and leave the generations to follow a piece of your legacy. Every year more people graduate school and are looking to fulfill their life's calling. Don't let your generation pass by without contributing. Life is more than working and earning a paycheck so you can party with what's left over after bills are paid. Don't be that shortsighted. Learn to discern the season you are in and perform that which is necessary for your success during that season.

50

CENTERED PEOPLE KNOW THEIR BATTLES

The Scripture states in Matthew 11:12 (NIV), *"From the days of John the Baptist until now, the kingdom of heaven has been forcefully advancing and forceful men lay hold of it."* Centered people know they can only go so far on their own strength. You have to fight and overcome by spiritual warfare, not fearing but determined you will attain all Christ has for you to attain. I have told people I am going to get mine. Satan isn't going to steal it. It is mine; I will fight until the death for it. People, who know me, understand this isn't a joke. My close friends have jokingly said that I'm a little high strung—wound a little tight. I have two speeds: fast and stop. At least I think they were joking. Anyway, they are right.

Derek Prince stated one time that God didn't call us to a playground but a battlefield. I don't think everything in life has to be full of battles; however, when taking back territory our fathers surrendered or we surrendered in our life, expect a fight. Just expect it. Then you won't feel sorry for yourself and whine, "Oh God, why me?" Instead you will be like the Twila Paris song, "The Warrior is a Child." The chorus states,

> They don't know that I go running home when I fall down.
> They don't know who picks me up when one is around.
> I drop my sword and cry for just a while.
> Cause deep inside this armor the warrior is a child.

Through the trials of life, we all experience hurt and pain and need God's love. Yes, we need to run to the father no matter how easy or hard the battle. He protects us and heals us. But we know that spiritual war is one that needs to be fought in order to take what is rightfully ours. In Colossians 2:15 (TAB) it states, *"God disarmed the principalities and powers that were ranged against us and made a bold display and public example of them, in triumphing over them in Him and in it the cross."*

God has won his war with Satan. Now you and I must win ours over Satan through the power of Jesus. Look at a couple more scriptures with me. Luke 10:19 (TAB) states, *"Behold I have given you authority and power to trample upon serpents and scorpions, and [physical and mental strength and ability] over all the power that the enemy [possesses]; and nothing shall in any way harm you."* That's part of what Christ paid the price for on the cross. He gave you and me his authority over all the power of the enemy. That's right, power over the serpents of lies and deceit, scorpions of sickness and disease. You know what you have to fight. Go fight it using the Word of God. Stake claim to what Christ bought for you. Make the enemy restore what he stole from you.

Matthew 18:18 (NIV), *"I tell you the truth , whatever you bind on earth will be bound in heaven, and whatever you loose on earth is loosed in heaven."* You have the authority to bind sickness, sin, disease, the voice of the accuser, and any work of the devil. The key to this verse is when it says "Whatever *you* bind." *You* have some binding and loosing to do. You ask, "What do I loose?" You need to loose a spirit of peace and health and protection on your family, loose ministering and warring angels to fight on your behalf. Loose the Word of God to do whatever it needs to do in your life right now in this season. Look at what Isaiah 55:11 (Msg) says about God's Word, *"So will the words that come out of my mouth not come back to me empty—handed. They'll do the work*

I sent them to do. They'll complete the assignment I gave them." The same verse in the New King James version states, *"So shall My word be that goes forth from my mouth; it shall not return void, but it shall accomplish what I please, And it shall prosper in the thing for which I sent it."* Your Bible is the God inspired and God spoken word. It is alive and vibrant. It has to do what *you* release it in faith to do in your life. This isn't some hocus pocus mumbo jumbo poem. It is real. Do you actually think the spiritual realm is shaken because you don't believe in it? They understand the matrix of dimensions God created and move on in spite of what we believe. They hold on to what they have stolen from you because you choose to not believe it.

We can influence that realm with our prayers. Remember, in the Garden Jesus said he willingly gave himself for us. He stated if he desired he could have asked his father to send thousands of angels at his disposal to save him from the cup he was being asked to fulfill. See Matthew 26:53 in the Living Bible. Instead, he chose to be obedient to his father for you and me. Where were those angels going to be dispatched from? Western Union? No, in the spirit world from a dimension in heaven. The Bible says God is light. My personal belief is that is why we can't see God. If his being is actually moving at the speed of light in constant motion to our eyes, no wonder we can't physically see him. That doesn't diminish his presence or existence. You may laugh or scoff at what I just wrote, but let me ask you something. What would have been easier for me? To not write about it and keep you from thinking I am off my rocker? Or, writing about it and giving you the scriptures to fight your fight and win what Christ rightfully has for you? I care enough for you to expose Satan for what he is. He is an accuser, a deceiver, thief, liar, and murderer. He has stolen enough lives and dreams through his lies. Determine he can no longer have yours.

I have had people tell me, "I have worked many years and hard and raised my family. Now it's time to retire and go down easy street." What they are telling me is that they are no longer a factor the devil has to worry about. It bothers me though because unless their children are in a happy, safe, vibrant marriage and successful careers and totally healed and overcome all the works of Satan in their lives then they aren't finished or ready for a retirement. We need to continue to fight for them as well. Don't be deceived. Proverbs 24:11–12 Living Bible states,

> Rescue those who are unjustly sentenced to death, don't stand back and let them die. Don't try to disclaim responsibility by saying you didn't know about it. For God who knows all hearts knows yours, and he knows you knew. And he will reward everyone according to his deeds.

So don't say, well my children are raised and aren't of concern to me now. They have their own battles to fight. It's all I can do to fight my own. Forbid that mindset and fight for them. Don't sit idly by and let them lose any area of their centered life. I actually know parents who don't want to see their children now that they are raised and out of the house. *Just because we don't see the spiritual world with physical eyes doesn't lessen its existence and power.* Fight for your children as well.

51

Centered People Learn to Discern the Voice of the Lord

Where were you on September 11, 2001? We all can certainly remember. I was up early packing for a flight to Dallas to interview for a different position at a hospital. My spirit was uneasy as I packed. I was debating with myself if I should change my flight from going through Philadelphia to Pittsburgh. It would allow me to arrive earlier and spend more time with my brother who lives in Dallas. As I wrestled with the decision, I also knew I hated flying. I flew through a storm one time and it knocked us out of our seats and people were screaming and yelling. I was petrified. I do remember a brother over my shoulder just reading the Bible not appearing to be bothered. I hated that flight and hated flying after that. So I thought my hesitancy was just fear of flying or, better put, fear of crashing.

As I was finishing packing, my son who was in the eighth grade came out of his room. He looked at me and said, "Dad I don't think you should go today, I don't have a good feeling about this."

I said, "Zachary we don't live life in fear; we press on." I hugged him and prayed and left. As I drove to the airport, my spirit wrestled like none before. I sat in front of the ticket counter and waited until the last minute, and I still didn't change my flight. I said, "Oh well, okay God I don't sense you giving me the okay." My spirit felt better but not total relief. As I ticketed and went up to the gate, I saw on the TV the first plane had already struck the world trade center building. I sat and had a coke and then witnessed the second plane flying into the second building. I turned to a man next to me and I said, "Did I just see that? Or was that film?" The news reporter then stated a second plane had just hit. I didn't wait for any announcements. I said, "Even as dumb as I am I am not flying today, job or no job, no matter how badly I want to leave where I am."

I soon learned about the plane going down outside of Pittsburgh. The place I was going to fly to. I would have been stuck in Pittsburgh and would have had to rent a car if possible and drive back to New York or have been stuck in Pittsburgh as they had shut down all air travel.

My point is to tell you how important it is to hear the Lord's voice or leading in situations. I was so proud to think that even my eighth grade son knew his spirit was telling him to tell me to not go. Man how I appreciate his innocence. I even further appreciate the Lord's faithfulness in my son's life as well. How thankful I was for all the men and women of God who helped teach my son in church and Sunday schools. They all contributed to that moment in saving our lives from either tragedy or extreme inconvenience. God is faithful.

I don't care what has happened in your life or mine. We live in a fallen world that fell when Adam and Eve sinned—simple as that. Let's not make it more complicated. As an ER nurse, I witnessed firsthand people dying who I thought would have lived. I witnessed people live who I thought would have died. It made no sense to me here in the natural realm. I saw firsthand God's fight for their soul as they left this earth. That's another book. I blamed God for things he didn't have anything to do with. I have seen people healed and I have experienced healing.

I have also seen people not totally healed. I have learned that God is first and foremost loving, just, faithful, kind, compassionate, longsuffering, and enduring forever. He is a just God. I have relieved myself of having to have all the answers. I can't be God in everyone's life. That's his responsibility. I am like Job. When Job questioned God, God's response in Job 38:4 (TLB), was *"Where were you when I laid the foundations of the earth?"* God proceeds to question Job and proves his point. I have often found that God doesn't answer many "why" questions.

You think Bathsheba's husband didn't have a few things to ask God? David had him murdered in a war so he could steal his wife. See 2 Samuel chapters 11 and 12. I bet Uriah said, "Wait a minute, what did I do to deserve this?" He possibly thought, "I lose my wife and my life?" Possibly wondering, "God how could you have allowed this to happen?" God disciplined David severely for his actions that day. David repented, and of course trouble followed David's whole household after that. David's sin caused many people pain they didn't deserve or bring on themselves.

Don't forget, God is so loving he gave his own son. He allowed his own son to die for all mankind. Since God did that, I think I shouldn't have any problems? That everything should be happy go lucky? Listen, I don't want to be cad but I want to grab your attention. God sent his own son. His own kid, his own love of his life! Jesus did nothing to deserve the sin thrust upon him by us. Get that in your mind and spirit. If I had been alive during those days, I would have reacted like everyone else. I would have sinned. It was God's best in exchange for my worst.

Most of the time we see things and live today in our own time, not in God's time. God's time is eternity. May I remind us that eternity doesn't start when you die. It started for each of us when God conceived us. You and I are living in eternity right now. Not tomorrow, but now. Have the mind of Christ concerning these matters.

Look at the conversation that took place between the thieves that were hung on each side of Jesus. Luke 23:39–43 (NLT) states,

> One of the criminals hanging beside him scoffed, So you're the Messiah, are you? Prove it by saving yourself-and us, too, while you're at it!" But the other criminal protested, "Don't you fear God even when you are dying? We deserve evil for our deeds, but this man <Jesus> hasn't done anything wrong." Then he said, "Jesus remember me when you come into your Kingdom." And Jesus replied, "I assure you, today you will be with me in paradise."

In other words, one challenged him saying if you really are the Son of God get us down out of here and deliver us. The other looked at him and said, "Shut up. We are getting what we deserve. Jesus doesn't deserve the punishment he is getting."

Jesus then looked at him and compassionately said, "Because you believed on me this day you will be with me in paradise." I wonder how old the unrepentant, mouthy thief felt after that? Remember, these were known thieves, convicted to die for thievery. They earned and deserved their convictions. Jesus didn't, and Jesus after having been beaten, scourged, spit on, kicked, whipped, brutally treated, and pierced, gave compassion. That was the greatest miracle he ever did in my opinion.

I haven't given compassion at times when I'm driving and get cut off by another driver. Look at what Jesus did and remember it was for us. It was for you and me and our families to follow. Jesus didn't look at him and say, "In case you haven't noticed I can't exactly breathe in this condition and you want me to perform a miracle?" Truth was, he was in the midst of doing the greatest miracle ever done. He was being rejected by his own father as being sin for us and was still being compassionate. That precious, special Lamb of God had his blood shed for us. How his father must have grieved for him as well, knowing he would be separated from his son for a period of time. I suggest as Christians we get used to some hardships and like Paul said, "…count it all blessing to suffer on the count of Jesus." I have felt at times I was knocking on heaven's door only to find I stared death in the face and smacked it twice. My father is so faithful! He truly is a father to the fatherless. I am not ashamed to be identified with him. Get to know your Lord and Savior better each day and count it all joy for the suffering he endured on the cross. For, after all, in comparison to eternity this is but a second. You can develop your spiritual sense to hear the direction and voice of the Lord.

HOWARD'S HELPFUL HINT: *Like Christ, a centered person doesn't take the easy way out of life. They pay the price.*

52

SPEAKING TO YOU FROM MY HEART

You may be like thousands of others who believe they have blown it or failed irreparably. That simply isn't true. I have been there. People just like you and me who cry themselves to sleep at night in hopelessness of shattered dreams feeling they can never get centered or never recover. Many others mentioned in the Bible have been used to show us that although they failed, God didn't leave them there in the failure. Remember, Moses and David both murdered. Adam and Eve disobeyed God's command, and we are paying the price for that to this day. Paul chased down Christians, some Bible versions state he hunted them down, and he held the cloaks of those murdering Stephen. Peter denied even knowing Christ more than once. Some denominations call Peter a saint. The disciples in their pride were caught arguing who would be the best instead of serving each other. They failed to even consider love that day. That is why we need Christ. None of us can make it without him. As you read earlier, I did things as a Christian I was ashamed of. I thought God could never and would never use me for anything worth anything. I then learned that God doesn't rank sin in an order. God doesn't consider murder worse than stealing or adultery worse than lying. God considers it all sin. When you broke one commandment, you broke them all. So you see when we sin, it is against God and only God. See Psalms 51. Our sin may affect others, but we sin against the one who labeled it all as sin. We, here on earth, have different consequences for different sins and crimes. But God doesn't. He lets us know in James that sin, when given full reign in our life, leads to death and separation from God in all areas. That's why I so desire you to live a centered life. He doesn't judge you as man judges you. The Bible says God is the Author and Finisher of our faith. I am so thankful he continues to finish the work he began in me.

You see, we aren't finished products yet so let's quit judging others and ourselves like this current state we are in is the best we will ever become. If you are in prison, God can use you there. If you are a recovering victim, God can heal you and use you even though your hour is at its darkest point. Remember, the scripture states that Jesus went to the pit of hell, bruised the serpent on the head, took the keys, unlocked the gates, and set the captives free. Christ has already been to hell for you. Since hell itself couldn't hold him back, what makes us think we can hold him back from anything in our lives? We can't limit or place God in a box. A box is too defining and limiting. There isn't one big enough, except the box in our minds. I pray you open the box of your mind and let God out to be the God he wants to be in your life.

> h³ **HOWARD'S HELPFUL HINT:** *Centered people have grown to know it is never too late for God.*

The circumstances may not turn out as we had hoped or imagined but it will still be okay for you. God hasn't let you go. I do understand maybe your marriage or business or family situation may not be able to be restored for whatever reason. That doesn't mean that *you* can't be restored. Don't forget what I mentioned earlier. The day both heaven and earth shook, God, our Father, took a thief off the cross into heaven with his son. As far as we know, that thief didn't keep any religious traditions and probably never tithed. Seems as if he was a taker, not a giver. But God met him right where he was and forgave him and cleansed him and honored him into heaven as his son had made a way for him. There is a fight for you and your soul until you breathe your last breath. I have witnessed this. God is still fighting on your behalf. He did his job by sending his son. We need to do ours now. Joel 2:13–14 (TLB) gives us all hope.

> Let remorse tear at your hearts and not your garments. Return to the Lord your God for he is gracious and merciful. He is not easily angered; he is full of kindness and anxious not to punish you. Perhaps he will let you alone and give you a blessing instead of a curse. Who knows? Perhaps he will give you so much that you can offer your grain and wine to the Lord as before.

I am not a biblical scholar, and I don't know what turned the people's hearts away from God. It appears they had even quit tithing. But look at what the scripture says about God's character and take hope. He is gracious, merciful, full of kindness, and anxious not to punish. He isn't hiding behind the bushes of life ready to jump out and "get you." Please get a different revelation of who God really is.

God even loved an unrepentant nation so much he had a prophet, Jonah, swallowed by a fish and regurgitated onto the shores of Ninevah so he could have his word delivered to bring repentance. The nation of Ninevah then did repent. Jonah was angry and didn't desire they repent, as he wanted them dealt with severely. But you see, God is not like us. Today, in this year you live in, he is still the same God. The Bible says *"God is the same yesterday, today, and forever"* (Hebrews 13:8, NLT). He never changes. That is why you can trust him. You can always depend on God to be who he says he is and to do what he says he will do. He doesn't change like we humans do. He isn't full of unstable emotions. He is the one stabilizing force in this universe he created. You see, he is the uncreated one. He doesn't have interchangeable parts to become different than he ever has been. He wants to and does exhibit all those characteristics towards you. I don't mean there aren't hard times. But I do mean that *God is always a good God! God is always forgiving and loving towards you, thinking good thoughts about you.* Read Psalms 139:17–18 in The Living Bible, *"How precious it is Lord to realize that you are thinking about me constantly. I can't even count how many times a day your thoughts turn towards me. And when I awaken in the morning you are still thinking of me."*

That should start your engine and excite you to know that the creator of all you see is constantly thinking of you. That's the kind of relationship he desires to have with you as the bride of Christ. Someone he is in love with, desiring to think about you often. It isn't in his nature to be any other way. Satan whispers in your ear that God isn't good towards others. He whispers lies like, old aunt so and so died when God could have helped her. This is to cause you to doubt.

Let me give you some insight. First of all, Satan is a liar and deceiver, that is his nature. His nature isn't like God's. Never trust the word of a coward like Satan. I say God doesn't have to be good towards Satan. God has to be *just* towards all creation. Why? Because that is God's nature. One more thing, let's quit placing Satan and God on the same pedestal. Satan can't even approach God without God's permission. He is too weak. Fear is his greatest weapon. I don't care what the Hollywood movies show you. Satan can't win out over God any more today than when Jesus humiliated him in front of the entire universe. Jesus already won! He is waiting for us to win with the power he gave us. He is enjoying participating in our lives as we live by faith in him. Jesus doesn't desire that any should perish but that all men should be saved to the glory of his father.

As the first part of Joel 2:13 states all you have to do is return to him. Pray and ask him in a simple prayer into your life and repent to the best of your knowledge of sin that is in your life. God will reveal the rest for you. He will cleanse you and restore you. He will cleanse the stains of guilt away from you as well. He wants you free to move forward.

Read Psalm 51:7 in TLB and take heart as David did. He said "...wash me and I will be whiter than snow." Even David, in his darkest hour, knew that any touch from God would be a total cleansing. David knew God's nature and David expected nothing less, even knowing he was undeserving. You see, unlike serving sin, serving God isn't bondage; it is life more abundantly. That goes against the teachings we have received about how God was going to get us if we weren't good. Sure there are consequences we must accept at times from society; however knowing that, we can still count on God's forgiving nature to cleanse us.

53

You Can Know Your Determined Purpose

What is your determined purpose?
In Philippians 3:10 (TAB) Paul stated, *"For my determined purpose is that I may know him that I may progressively become more deeply and intimately acquainted with him, perceiving and recognizing and understanding the wonders of his person more strongly and more clearly. And in that same way come to know the out flowing from his resurrection."* The Bible states you can have a determined purpose. Like Paul, I am at a time in my life where Philippians 3:10 is my determined purpose.

I desire more of the fruit spoken of in Galatians 5. I desire to develop more joy, more faith, more love. I desire to develop more of God's characteristics in my life. I desire a deeper, more graceful walk with and in Jesus. I want to understand who I am in Jesus. I want to identify with him and clothe myself with Jesus and with his grace. I want his very life to flow out through me to others. I don't really care about the rest this world has to offer. I also know there is a price to be paid for this adventure. It isn't easy. I wouldn't know how to respond if it was easy. Look at 2 Peter 1: 3 (TLB): *"Do you want to know more and more of God's peace? Then learn to know him better and better. For as you know him better, He will give you, through his great power, everything you need to live a truly good life."*

> **h³** HOWARD'S HELPFUL HINT: *Centered people learn to know God better and better.*

You can become a single-minded person that is stable and focused on God and his ways. Your feet will be placed on a firm path. You can be grounded and planted in a church, becoming a new person in all the ways you do and think. You will be like Paul in Philippians 3:13–14 (TAB), *"Brethren I do not count myself to apprehend but one thing I do, forgetting those things which are behind and reaching forward to those things which are ahead, I press toward the goal for the prize of the upward call of God in Christ Jesus."* You can leave the past behind and actively pursue a new life, no matter how much time you have left on this earth. Remember I explained you are already in eternity.

In Jeremiah 33:3 (NKJV), God guarantees he will answer you. It states, *"Call unto me and I will answer you and show you great and mighty things which you do not know."* Your destination and life will change when you leave the earth in spirit. Don't be frightened of it, but be excited reaching forward. On his website, a man who has a ministry that totally blesses me is Casey Treat. I encourage you to visit it. His testimony from jail to where he is today is powerful. In his daily devotion once he said, "Faith doesn't wait for everyone else. Today don't worry about those around you. They may or may not go for it, but I will live my own life with the Lord and fulfill my own destiny in him. I won't compare myself to others." When I first read that I was so encouraged to know I could go for it and not worry about what others may do or think of me. I also didn't need permission nor did I have to wait on everyone else. It was such a release for me.

I realized nothing could hold me back unless I let it. I actively threw off the self-imposed restraints I had allowed to be placed on me by others and myself. I became a new person by doing that. May God bless his ministry.

54

BECOME THE CENTERED PERSON
GOD IS CALLING YOU TO BE

I wrote this book out of a desire God placed in my heart to invest in his most precious creation and resource, people. You see, when Christ died, we weren't even born yet in the physical realm. Yet, God still saw us and had a plan for us. That plan was to live as an unblemished and pure and holy people. This is all about becoming. It is not about achieving and finally getting there, no matter wherever "there" happens to be. God has not called us to do or be something that he knows we aren't equipped for. He always gives us the grace necessary. You have a choice of actions to make. One is *responding* to Christ, which is a choice; the other is *reacting,* which is an emotional reflex. I don't ever want to say, "Well I am old, I have finished the race, now I can die and go to the sweet bye and bye." You say well that's what the disciple Paul did. Let me correct your thinking. Paul was *called* home *after* he finished his race. He didn't sit back until Christ returned. He didn't *retire* and then go *home.* He didn't look at all his accomplishments in the Lord and decide to live on easy street. I want to keep being centered by getting to know Christ and live with him daily. That is his desire for you and me. Like Paul and the other disciples, we too will finish our race by becoming more and more Christ-like.

In my life, Christ has dulled the edge of what I was, taking the sharpness away and re-sharpening me into whom he has desired me to be. He tempered me through the cleansing fires of life and helped me learn to handle life intelligently. I had to detach from the results this world had to offer to do a work that wouldn't allow me to rest until it was finished. This has been a good thing in my life, and as you allow God to work in your life it will be for you as well.

Please take this book and invest in yourself and others the concepts God has revealed to me to give to you. Help me be the steward God has called me to be. Press on in the faith.

I hope I get to meet all of you who read this and are inspired by the revelations. Be encouraged by this scripture that is very fitting for the world in which we live today:

I Peter 1:2 (TLB) states,

> God the Father chose you long ago and knew you would become his children. And the Holy Spirit has been at work in your hearts, cleansing you with the blood of Jesus Christ and making you to please him. May God bless you richly and grant you increasing freedom from all anxiety and fear.

Your friend,
Howard

Final Chapter

ONLY FOR THE STRONG AND ENDURING

This next chapter is only for the strong that desire to keep pressing on. The scripture states that to whom much is given much is expected. Oftentimes, we think in the natural that when we prosper financially much is expected of us. While that is true, it is even truer in the spiritual realm. When we are given insight and revelation into certain areas or we gain victory in spiritual warfare, God expects us to be great stewards of that. I have friends who inherited their parents business and act like they really paid the price, when in reality it was their parents who paid the price for where that business is today and handed down to their son or daughter to be a great steward of it. I only respect those who were given the business and made it more than it was when they received it. God is the same with us. It cost God his son and a lot of pain to give us what he has given us. He gives us everything as stewards of his gifts and resources and is counting on us to make it better than when we first received it. Is your relationship with God better than it was when you were first saved? Have you been a good steward of it? I also see this in pastors who started churches with nothing but a dream and vision. They met in rented rooms and small old churches and now meet in thousand-seat auditoriums. Those are faithful stewards. I have paid a big price to attain what God has given me, and I don't intend to give it up that easy and not steward it.

> **HOWARD'S HELPFUL HINT:** *Centered people steward the things given them to a greater status than when they first received them.*

It is a privilege to have been given anything from God. I remember Frank Sinatra singing; he did it his way. I want to sing; I did it God's way. Is that your desire as well? I can look up at the stars and talk to the one who created it all. Why then would I swoon over a celebrity? I know the creator of it all. I say this without arrogance. I have met lots of celebrities, and I don't see myself different than they are. They aren't better than me, nor am I better than them. I know and try to introduce the creator to them all. My point is that we need to be stewards of all the relationships God has given us. That's doing it God's way.

I have had a lot of conversations with God, seeking answers as to who he really is. I don't want the American version, the Methodist, Baptist, Catholic, German, European, or any other version. I want to know who he truly is. I desire God's version! I want to know why he still allowed Moses to deliver his people after Moses committed murder. Is it perhaps it wasn't the same Moses after forty years away? God's wisdom and sovereignty is so great. His love and mercy are so enduring.

I have been through the fire of life as I write this. I have been left wondering at times if it is all for naught. I have had those closest to me reject my values and my love. I have experienced the pain and loneliness of friends and loved ones walking away from me, saying lies about me, slandering me. I have found that God still requires me to love them. When one of our loved ones goes through a period in life where we feel justified if we cut our ties with them or get divorced or just completely cut off the relationship with them, we need to think again. Just because a loved one goes through trials and leaves the faith for a bit, doesn't relieve us of still doing the right thing. Notice, I didn't say the comfortable thing or popular thing or what we want to do. We are obligated to love with the fruit of the spirit God gives us—that is to love our neighbor as ourself. So few Christians get to live this out because they choose not to. I have chosen to embrace the scripture and be as obedient as I know to be. I'm not perfect; I have my moments and failures too. However, it still is a choice we all have to make. We may be able to justify cutting off the relationship, but can we justify to God why we didn't love them, as we would have wanted someone to love us? We want God to forgive us and love us and take us back, but we don't want to do the same for brothers and sisters who stumble. I know this isn't easy. But who takes the easy way out of everything? We worry too much about our pride and our image or reputation. Let's lay it all down and *love* those around us. I still have much to learn in this area. But trust me when I say God is making sure I learn it now. Some of the situations are too personal for me to write in this book. But the scripture says that what we go through is common to man. So we can rest assured that we aren't the only ones to be facing or to have ever faced this situation we find ourselves in, regardless of how we feel or want to believe. I have no choice but to trust God and not quit now. Remember what I shared earlier. God will never leave us nor forsake us. Our friends might, our bodies will, this old world surely will, b*ut God won't!* If nothing else, always remember God is faithful. When everything else and everyone else isn't, God is! I mentioned in an earlier chapter, the Twila Paris song, "The Warrior Is A Child;" I embrace that song as if it were written for me. After I have shared the pain and struggles I have faced with those close to me, my friends have told me that they see me as a warrior, strong, brave, courageous, fighting the fight where others won't. But what they don't see is when I run to my father in tears, hurt, angry, tired, wanting to quit, saying it isn't worth it. I have faced that place many times in my life. God told me he hurts when his children quit after all he has done for them. They reject him and his ways in ignorance and fear. After he *gave* his son, why is it we quit so easily? Yes, I do mean easily. I think it is because we haven't touched the breadth of what he *really* did for us. *It is a real powerful event that occurred on our behalf.* God allowed the precious blood of his son to be spilled on my behalf. And I quit? Sounds like grow up time to me. I hear people say this or that person just needs to get tough. I disagree; I don't like tough meat. I like strong, healthy meat. I choose strong over tough any day. God never called me to be tough or perfect; he called me to be *his!* He has called you as well.

Just like you, I am currently laboring in areas wondering how it all will turn out. Not knowing that answer causes us to live a life of faith. This much I do know, God will make sure it all works out for his glory. He will share his glory with no one but his church. I have seen this time and time again. We won't be able to say, "Well this guy or that guy saved me out of that hard time." Oh yes, God will use us and other people to help people during trials in their lives, but we will boast that God, and only God, could have saved us out of the fires of life and into something great. We survived and conquered because of him and him only! Wow, what a testimony to the great cloud of witnesses who also saw their faith rewarded when they wanted to retreat yet chose not to. We will join them as a conquering body.

Live in love, live in strength, and be encouraged;
most of all, live centered!

Endnotes

1 {See Address to graduating class of Wheaton College May 9, 1993}

2 \<See GQ December 2004>

To contact Howard for speaking engagements and consultations, please visit his website: www.howardlull.com